Seven Habits
Of an Effective Prayer Life

A nine session small group experience

Second Edition

Alvin J. Vander Griend

7710-T Cherry Park Dr, Ste 224
Houston, TX 77095
(713) 766-4272

Copyright © 2016 by Alvin J. Vander Griend

All Scripture quotations not otherwise designated are from the HOLY BIBLE, NEW INTERNATIONAL VERSION®. NIV®. Copyright © 1973, 1978, 1984 by International Bible Society. Used by permission of Zondervan. All rights reserved worldwide.

Contents of this handbook may be reprinted with permission from Alvin J. Vander Griend
    E-mail: Alvin@harvestprayer.com

7710-T Cherry Park Dr, Ste 224
Houston, TX 77095
(713) 766-4272

Paperback: ISBN 978-0692621400

Also by Alvin J. Vander Griend

Passion and Power in Prayer

The Praying Church Sourcebook with Edith Bajema

Patterns for Prayer

Discover Your Gifts and Learn How to Use Them

Be Jesus in Your Neighborhood

Shine His Light

There's Hope, Living by the Book

40 Days of Prayer, Strategy Guidelines

Love to Pray

The Joy of Prayer

Praying God's Heart

Table of Contents

Preface 7

A Word to Course Participants 8

Session 1

    Be Devoted to Prayer 11

Session 2

    Habit One: *Claim God's Riches* 19

Session 3

    Habit Two: *Give God Glory* 27

Session 4

    Habit Three: *Seek God's Face* 37

Session 5

    Habit Four: *Win over Sin* 45

Session 6

    Habit Five: *Hear God's Voice* 53

Session 7

    Habit Six: *Pray for Family and Friends in Christ* 63

Session 8

    Habit Seven: *Pray for Neighbors and Nations* 73

Session 9

    Be a Prayer-Devoted Church 83

Appendices

About the Course

    Goals and Values of the Course 92

    Honing Your Prayer Habits 94

    Finding an Affinity Prayer Group 97

    Becoming a Prayer-Devoted Church 101

    Bonus Follow-Up Session 105

Leader Helps

    How to Use this Course. 107

    Forming a *Seven Habits* Class 108

    Leading a *Seven Habits* Class 109

Personal Guides

    Prayer Guide and Scripture Memory Guide 112

Preface

This course, *Seven Habits of an Effective Prayer Life*, will not give you seven easy steps to success in prayer. The prayer habits we are talking about are incredibly valuable, even life-changing, but they are not easy. Many things in our lives compete with our efforts to develop good prayer habits: busy schedules, old prayer habits, lack of discipline, misuse of media, and the devil himself. However, weak prayer habits and competing influences can be overcome; and because prayer involves us in life's most important relationship, overcoming these challenges is worth all the effort that it will take.

This course is not designed to change your theology of prayer, though that may happen. It is rather designed to change the less-than-satisfying way that many of us relate to God on a day-to-day basis. It's intended to help you find new ways to pray and to lock in habits that will deepen your faith, stimulate spiritual growth, increase your fruitfulness, and draw you closer to God.

Nor is this course meant to increase the amount of time you spend in prayer, though that too may happen. As a participant, you will be encouraged to spend generous amounts of time in prayer; but it's not the amount of time that is most important. What is more important is what you actually do in prayer. The prayer habits of Old and New Testament saints and the example of Christ himself will set the standards by which you can evaluate your own personal prayer habits. Many Scripture passages will challenge you with calls to prayer that come from the heart of God.

Finally, what you take away from this course must be *you:* your way of understanding prayer, your spiritual journey, and your love relationship with God. You may end up adding some new prayer habits to those you already practice. You may use the suggested prayer habits in a way that is totally unique to you. You may diminish the time you spend in some of the habits and increase the amount of time you spend with others. None of us relates to God in exactly the same way.

What the course is designed to give you are biblically based building blocks by which you can cultivate an increasingly effective prayer life and reap the resulting harvest of spiritual blessings. It is my hope and prayer that you will find, as I have, that good prayer habits will help you be the pray-er God wants you to be, and will enable you to "pray in the Spirit on all occasions with all kinds of prayer and requests . . . and always keep on praying for all the saints" (Eph. 6:18).

Alvin J. Vander Griend

A Word to Course Participants

Before each class session:

- First, read the **Introduction** to the session you are preparing. Mark words, sentences or thoughts that strike you as particularly important. Note any questions you may have.

- Next, work through the **Bible Study**. Thoughtfully read through the Scripture passages in a subsection. Mark the ideas that stand out to you. Think about the truths in the passages as you answer the Discover/Reflect/Apply questions.

    - **Discover** questions are answerable directly from the Scripture passages.
    - **Reflect** questions invite you to ponder the truths in the Scripture passages more deeply.
    - **Apply** questions invite you to think through ways that the Bible truths apply to you personally. **[Mark the questions that provided the best insights for you.]**

- Summarize your thoughts with the **Bottom Line Questions** and read the **Summing Up** thoughts at the end of the study.

During each class session:

- Be prepared to share insights with your group based on the **discover/reflect/apply** questions, and to learn from the contributions of others.

- Work through the personal elements in "**Four Steps to Develop a Prayer Habit**" as carefully as possible.

- Challenge yourself to contribute to **group prayer** - even if you find this hard to do. It gets easier as you go.

- Make the **Whole Group Covenant** with your group and do your best to keep it.

Between class sessions:

- **Pray for Each Other.** Release God's power and grace into each other's lives by praying daily for the members of your group.

- **Practice the Habits.** Practice the prayer habit of the week every day between the sessions. Try to give each habit five or more minutes each day. Continue to practice previously learned prayer habits.

- Review **Ways to Develop the Habit** to find some additional ways to work at a prayer habit.

- Consider using the *Seven Habits* **Prayer Guide** and **Scripture Memory Guide** (see the appendix) to help you lock in good prayer habits.

SESSION 1

Be Devoted to Prayer

God wants every one of us to be devoted to prayer. Jesus was clearly devoted to prayer. He often prayed early in mornings, at the end of long days, and sometimes all through the night. He prayed in solitary places, on mountainsides, in the wilderness, and in a garden. He prayed at nearly every major milestone of his life. The gospels record eighteen references to Jesus' prayer life, fourteen different teachings on prayer themes, and eight actual prayers.

The apostle Paul was so devoted to prayer that he spent, as one writer put it, "as much time on his knees as on his feet." Twelve times in his letters Paul reports how constantly he thanks God for his readers and prays for them. Nine times he reports what he is praying for them. And six times he either asks for others to pray for him or reports on answers to their prayers for him.

The first Christians were also devoted to prayer. Six times New Testament writers use the intense Greek word *proskartereo,* which literally means "strongly toward," to speak of believers' commitment to prayer. In five of the six locations (Eph. 6:18 is the exception) the New American Standard Bible uses the word "devote" to translate *proskartereo*, thus underscoring the reality that the apostles were "devoted to prayer" (Acts 6:4 NASB), that believers of the Jerusalem Church were "devoted to prayer" (Acts 1:14, 2:42 NASB), and that all Christians are commanded to be "devoted to prayer" (Rom. 12:12, Col. 4:2 NASB). In addition to the word "devote," the Bible regularly uses words like "bold," "earnest," "persistent," "constant," "wrestling," "day and night," and "non-stop" to describe the prayers and prayer habits of early believers. What could be clearer?

Prayer is vital because it is the tangible way we live out our love relationship with the Father, Son and Holy Spirit. Prayer is also imperative because God accomplishes his work on earth in response to the prayers of his people. Though God is almighty, all-wise, and fully able to work without us, he chooses to act in response to prayer, and often desists when there is little or no prayer. The Spirit's command to early believers is still valid today: "Devote yourselves to prayer, being watchful and thankful" (Col. 4:2).

As you study the following Scripture passages, I challenge you to compare your prayer life to that of Jesus and Paul, and to compare your church's prayer life to that of the New Testament church. Step into the friend-in-the-middle role of Jesus' parable, or imagine yourself being an "Epaphras" for your church. Do it, not out of duty, but out of love for Jesus. Do it, not out of human strength, but in the power of the Holy Spirit.

Bible Study for "Devoted to Prayer"

Note that all italics below were inserted by the author of this study.

Jesus Devotion to Prayer

[When it comes to prayer, Jesus is the perfect example.]

Very early in the morning, while it was still dark, Jesus got up, left the house, and went off to a solitary place, where *he prayed*. –Mk. 1:35

After leaving them, [Jesus] went up on a *mountainside to pray*. –Mk. 6:46

The news about [Jesus] spread all the more, so that crowds of people came to hear him and to be healed of their sicknesses. But Jesus often *withdrew* to lonely places *and prayed*. –Luke 5:15-16

One of those days Jesus went out to a mountainside to pray, and *spent the night praying* to God. –Luke 6:12

And being in anguish, he *prayed more earnestly*, and his sweat was like drops of blood falling to the ground. –Luke 22:44

After Jesus said this, he looked toward heaven and *prayed*. –John 17:1

Discover
- What features of Jesus' prayer life do you notice in these verses?

- If you had to characterize Jesus' prayer life in one word, what would that word be?

Reflect
- Do you think that Jesus was *drawn* to pray or *driven* to pray? What might have drawn him? What might have driven him?

- To what extent did Jesus' prayer life contribute to the success of his ministry?

Apply
- When it comes to prayer, what does it mean to be Christ-like?

- How might your life be different if you had a prayer life like that of Jesus?

- What do you need to do in order to find more alone-time with God?

Believers Devoted to Prayer

These all [the disciples and others who witnessed Jesus' ascension] with one mind were continually *devoting themselves to prayer*, along with the women, and Mary the mother of Jesus, and with His brothers. –Acts 1:14 (NASB)

They were continually *devoting* themselves to the apostles' teaching and to fellowship, to the breaking of bread and *to prayer*. –Acts 2:42 (NASB)

On their release, Peter and John went back to their own people and reported all that the chief priests and the elders had said to them. When they heard this, they *raised their voices together in prayer* to God. –Acts 4:23-24

"But we will *devote* ourselves *to prayer* and to the ministry of the word." –Acts 6:4 (NASB)

So Peter was kept in prison, but the church was *earnestly praying* to God for him. –Acts 12:5

Discover
- What is there about the prayer lives of these New Testament Christians that really stands out?

- Based on these verses, how would you define devotion to prayer?

Reflect
- Do you think their prayers arose from desperation or desire? Explain.

- What are some of the things they prayed about?

- What did they apparently believe about prayer? What were they thinking about Jesus when they prayed?

Apply
- What would move you to be more devoted to prayer?

- What have you learned about prayer from these verses that might apply to your local church?

Commands to be Devoted to Prayer

"But I tell you: Love your enemies and *pray* for those who persecute you." –Matt. 5:44

"Watch and *pray* that you will not fall into temptation." –Matt. 26:41

Rejoicing in hope, persevering in tribulation, *devoted to prayer*. –Rom. 12:12 (NASB)

And *pray* in the Spirit *on all occasions* with all kinds of prayers and requests. With this in mind, be alert and *always keep on praying* for all the Lord's people. –Eph. 6:18

Devote yourselves *to prayer*, keeping alert in it with an attitude of thanksgiving. –Col. 4:2 (NASB)

"Rejoice always, *pray continually*, give thanks in all circumstances; for this is God's will for you in Christ Jesus." –1 Thess. 5:16-18

Discover
- Describe in your own words the role that God intends prayer to have in our lives.

- What makes it possible for us to pray "on all occasions" (Eph. 6:18)?

- What other spiritual actions are linked with devotion to prayer?

Reflect
- What does it mean to pray "on all occasions" (Eph. 6:18)?

- Why do you think we are challenged to "watch" and "be alert" in these passages?

Apply
- If it is God's will for us to be devoted to prayer, what should we do if we find ourselves failing?

- What "occasions" in your life are most likely to trigger prayer?

- What would be happening in your relationship with God if you prayed "on all occasions with all kinds of prayer"?

Examples of Devotion to Prayer

(Nehemiah) "When I heard these things, I sat down and wept. For some days I mourned and *fasted and prayed* before the God of heaven. Then I said: 'LORD, the God of heaven, the great and awesome God, who keeps his covenant of love with those who love him and keep his commandments, let your ear be attentive and your eyes open to *hear the prayer* your servant is praying before you day and night for your servants, the people of Israel. I confess the sins we Israelites, including myself and my father's family, have committed against you.'" –Neh. 1:4-6

Elijah was a human being, even as we are. He *prayed earnestly* that it would not rain, and it did not rain on the land for three and a half years. Again he prayed, and the heavens gave rain, and the earth produced its crops. –James 5:17-18

(Paul) "I thank God, whom I serve, as my ancestors did, with a clear conscience, as *night and day I constantly remember you in my prayers.*" –2 Tim. 1:3

Discover
- What words in these passages make the intensity of their prayers vivid?

- What did Nehemiah think of God?

Reflect
- How do our thoughts about God affect our prayer lives?

- Why does James underscore the fact that Elijah was a human being, just like us?

- What difference did Paul's prayers for Timothy make in the church world?

Apply
- What do you believe about God that encourages you to pray?

- Is God doing things in the world today because you are praying? If so, what?

Bottom Line Questions
1. What is the most important idea you are taking away from this *devoted-to-prayer* study?

2. What, practically, could you do to become more *devoted to prayer*?

Summing Up

It's amazing, that Scripture uses so many superlative words when it talks about prayer: "always," "all occasions," "day and night," "earnest," "bold," "wrestling," "devoted," "constantly," "not stopped," "every time" and "persistent." This is the way we might talk about a championship football team. But Scripture is talking about praying people—people devoted to prayer, people with good prayer habits.

The Bible verses we have studied tell us not only about prayer but about God. Prayer is first of all God's thing. He commands it, he expects it, and he works in response to it. Devotion to prayer is devotion to God. It's a way of relating to God and honoring his way of working in the world.

Don't forget as you go on that devotion to prayer is more than knowledge of prayer or commitment to prayer. Prayer is an activity. You can't be devoted to prayer without doing it, any more than you can be devoted to golf if you never swing a club. Elijah, Jesus, Paul and the early church believers had good habits of prayer. Their devotion to prayer took the form of habitually doing it. They actually did pray on all occasions with all kinds of prayers and requests . . . and always kept on praying for all God's people. There is no other way to be devoted to prayer.

Four Steps to Becoming a Prayer-Devoted Christian

1. Set the Stage for Becoming More Devoted to Prayer
- Let God speak to you through Ephesians 6:18. Tell God what you are going to do with it. Mark key words or thoughts. Prepare yourself to memorize it.
  "And pray in the Spirit on all occasions with all kinds of prayers and requests. With this in mind, be alert and always keep on praying for all the Lord's people." –Eph. 6:18
- Set some goals:
  - How much time are you willing to commit each day in order to become a person devoted to prayer? (_____)
  - What less valuable activities are you willing to give up to make more time for prayer? (_____)
  - How many times a day would you like to pause and talk to God about something? (_____)

2. Detect Habits That May Hinder Your Being Devoted to Prayer
Which of the following habits may hinder your *devotion to prayer*?
  ___ I haven't taken God's command to be devoted to prayer very seriously.
  ___ I'm afraid that I haven't built enough time into my schedule for devotion to prayer.
  ___ I have not asked the Spirit's help to pray "on all occasions with all kinds of prayer" (Eph. 6:18).
  ___ Prayer tends to be for me more a duty than a delight.
  ___ I am probably less devoted to prayer than to some less-worthy earthly things.

3. Launch Yourself into a Lifestyle of Devotion to Prayer

- *Thank* God for giving you prayer as a way to live in a love relationship with him, and to advance the cause of his kingdom in the world today. *Thank* God for the way he has helped you develop your prayer life so far.
- *Confess* any hindrances to prayer devotion (from step 2 above) and turn them around.
- *Ask* God to help you become truly devoted to prayer.
- *Commit* yourself to a lifestyle of full devotion to prayer.

4. Lock In a Lifestyle of Devotion to Prayer

⇒ Start each day asking God for a more devoted prayer life. That's a prayer God is eager to answer.
⇒ Build prayer into your day by writing "meet God" in your day planner to identify your devotional time(s).
⇒ Review periodically the Scripture passages from the Bible study section and recommit yourself to God's high standard for prayer.
⇒ Review how well you did in prayer at the end of each day. Celebrate the gains. Repent the missed opportunities.

Group Prayer and Covenant Time

The Entire Group Prepares for and Prays Personal Prayers of Confession and Petition

- Each person selects one **hindering habit**—one you marked in step 2 above—to bring to the whole group prayer time.
- Group members **take one minute** to consider the negative effects of that hindrance and reflect on (or write down) what positive change to ask God for:

_____

_____

- Each person contributes a **two-sentence prayer**: one sentence to confess the hindering habit, and a second sentence to claim God's grace to develop a "right" habit. (Leaders go first.)

The Whole Group Covenants Together Aloud and In Unison

"In utter dependence upon Jesus Christ as my ever-living Savior, Teacher, Lord and prayer partner, I will devote myself to prayer and will faithfully support the others in our Seven Habits group in their pursuit of effective prayer habits."

Small Group Share and Prayer Time
(The session ends with this exercise.)

- Each person writes down:
A prayer request for the help you need to be more ***devoted to prayer:***

  _____
  _____

  Another prayer request for yourself or for one other person:

  _____
  _____

- Each person shares, in two or three sentences, the above two prayer requests with their small group of 2-4 persons.

- Each person prays for one other person in the group covering the two requests just shared.

AFTER SESSION ONE

Pray for Each Other
Pray for the members of your group, especially your small group, every day with the understanding that things will happen in their prayer lives if you pray for them that won't happen if you don't pray.

Pray about Your Prayer Life
Review key Scripture passages from session one. Pray about your own devotion to prayer. Watch carefully for God's leadings. Is he showing you what pleases him about your prayer life? Teaching you about deficiencies in prayer? Giving you an increased desire for prayer? Giving you a better understanding of prayer?

Increase Your Devotion to Prayer

◊ Pray about prayer. Start each day asking God for a more devoted prayer life. That's a prayer God is eager to answer.

◊ Ask the Spirit to alert you to the occasions in which he wants you to be praying "with all kinds of prayers and requests." At the end of each prayer occasion, ask the Spirit to prompt you at the next possible prayer opportunity.

◊ Invite God to wake you up sometime in the middle of the night for prayer. Promise him that, if he does, you will pray for the things he puts on your heart.

SESSION 2

Habit One: **Claim God's Riches**

To "claim God's riches" is to ask God for the spiritual riches that he wants to give to us, his children. The Bible is full of verses encouraging us to ask for ourselves. Jesus said, "*Ask [for yourselves]** whatever you wish, and it will be done for you" (John 15:7). John stressed that "if we *ask [for ourselves]** anything according to his [God's] will, he hears us. And if we know that we hears us—whatever we ask—we know that we have what we asked of him" (1 John 5:14-15).

These verses are not urging us to ask for anything we might want, with the expectation that God will deliver on cue. Rather, they are inviting us to ask for things that God, in his infinite wisdom and love, wants to give in response to our asking. These are blessings that will enrich, strengthen and beautify our lives. These are the things he knows we need, the things that are truly good for us. Our spiritual well-being is tied to our asking and receiving God's heavenly gifts. No one has a greater responsibility to pray for you than you.

Asking for God's good gifts for ourselves is not selfish. It is, in fact, the way for us to grow in grace and to become Christ-like. "Whether we like it or not," said C. H. Spurgeon, "asking is the rule of the kingdom." God delights in our asking because we are his children. His Father-heart leaps for joy when we ask for what he wants to give us. Asking for ourselves underscores the reality that we are God's dependent children and that he is our all-sufficient Father.

James said to spiritually impoverished New Testament believers, "You do not have because you do not ask God" (Jas. 4:2). Could James's critique explain why there is so much spiritual poverty today? Would we not have more wisdom, more power, more love, more joy, more peace, more grace, and more of "all that pertains to life and godliness" if we regularly asked? Is that why Jesus urged us to pray for ourselves: "Ask and it will be given you, seek and you will find, knock and the door will be opened to you"? Did he know that we would stumble and fall if we didn't claim God's riches?

God has made incredible promises to us in the hopes that we will ask and receive what he knows we need. God will be disappointed, and we will be the poorer, if we do not ask. Theresa of Avila once declared, "You pay God a great compliment by asking great things of him." What are you going to ask?

---

*When a verb in the Greek is in the middle voice, as these verbs are, it means that the subject is acting for him/herself. The authors were saying that the pray-ers were "asking for themselves."

Bible Study for "Claim God's Riches"

Note that all italics below were inserted by the author of this study.

We *Should* Claim God's Riches

This is the confidence we have in approaching God: that if we *ask [for ourselves]* anything according to his will, he hears us. And if we know that he hears us -- whatever we *ask [for ourselves]* -- we know that we have what we asked of him.
–1 John 5:14-15

"Ask and it will be given to you; seek and you will find; knock and the door will be opened to you. For everyone who asks receives; the one who seeks finds; and to the one who knocks, the door will be opened." –Matt. 7:7-8

"Call to me and I will answer you and *tell you* great and unsearchable things you do not know." –Jer. 33:3

Discover
- What is the main thing we must do in order to personally receive spiritual riches from God?

- What can we "know" for sure if we ask in accord with God's will?

Reflect
- What can we learn about God from these verses? What do these verses tell us about human beings?

- Why do you think God wants us to *ask* for things that he wants us to have? Why doesn't he just give them to us (1 Jn. 5:14-15)?

- If we don't ask, will God withhold from us things he knows we need, things he really wants us to have?

- How will regularly asking for and receiving spiritual riches from God affect our spiritual lives?

Apply
- What are the three top things you want to receive from God?

- Share with the group, if you can, a time when you asked for something in accord with God's will and got what you asked for.

What Riches We Should Claim

"If you, then, though you are evil, know how to give good gifts to your children, how much more will your Father in heaven give *good gifts* to those who ask him!" –Matt. 7:11

Do not be anxious about anything, but in every situation, by prayer and petition, with thanksgiving, present your requests to God. And the *peace of God*, which transcends all understanding, will guard your hearts and your minds in Christ Jesus. –Phil. 4:6-7

Let us then approach God's throne of grace with confidence, so that we may receive *mercy* and find *grace* to help us in our time of need. –Heb. 4:16

If any of you lacks *wisdom*, you should ask God, who gives generously to all without finding fault, and it will be given to you. –James 1:5

Discover
- Name the good gifts mentioned in these verses that God is willing and able to give to those who ask.

- What kinds of life situations does God want to help us overcome by means of His good gifts?

Reflect
- What do we learn about God in these verses that gives us the confidence to ask Him for good gifts?

- Should we encourage non-believers that we know to ask for these good gifts from God?

Apply
- If you are aware of having received good gifts from God in response to your asking, share one such experience with your group. (Matt. 7:11)

- What will happen in your spiritual life if you regularly ask for and receive God's good gifts? What will happen if you don't ask?

Conditions for Claiming God's Riches

Take delight in the L ORD, and he will give you the desires of your heart. –Psalm 37:4

"Because *he loves me*," says the L ORD, "I will rescue him; I will protect him, for *he acknowledges* my name. He will call on me, and I will answer him; I will be with him in trouble, I will deliver him and honor him."
–Ps. 91:14-15

"If you *remain in me* and *my words remain in you*, ask [for yourselves] whatever you wish, and it will be done for you."
–John 15:7

Dear friends, if our hearts do not condemn us, we have confidence before God and receive from him anything we ask, because we *keep his commands* and *do what pleases him*.
–1 John 3:21-22

If any of you lacks wisdom, you should ask God, who gives generously to all without finding fault, and it will be given to you. But when you ask, you *must believe and not doubt*, because the one who doubts is like a wave of the sea, blown and tossed by the wind.
–James 1:5-6

Discover
- List as many conditions for getting what you ask for in prayer as you can find in these verses.

- In what six ways, according to Psalm 91:14-15, will God respond to those who love him and call on him?

Reflect
- Why is God eager to grant the desires of those who meet the conditions mentioned here?

- Why is God not inclined to answer the prayers of those who do not meet the conditions?

- Is it possible for believers to actually meet these conditions for answered prayer? If so, how?

Apply
- Which of these conditions comes most easily for you?

- Which condition is hardest for you to meet?

An Example of Claiming God's Riches

(Solomon) "Give me *wisdom and knowledge*, that I may lead this people, for who is able to govern this great people of yours?"

God said to Solomon, "Since this is your heart's desire and you have not asked for wealth, possessions or honor, nor for the death of your enemies, and since you have not asked for a long life but for wisdom and knowledge to govern my people over whom I have made you king, therefore wisdom and knowledge will be given you. And I will also give you wealth, riches and honor, such as no king who was before you ever had and none after you will have." –2 Chron. 1:10-12

Discover
- Why did Solomon ask for wisdom and knowledge? What else might he have asked for?

Reflect
- Why do you think God was so ready to grant Solomon's request for wisdom? Why was he willing to even go beyond Solomon's request?

- What does Solomon's request for wisdom and knowledge teach you about asking for yourself?

- Is what God offers to New Testament Christians today more or less than he offered to Solomon? Explain.

Apply
- If God offered to give you whatever you wanted, what would you ask for?

Bottom Line Questions
1. What is the single most important idea you are taking away from this *claim-God's-riches* study?

2. What, practically, might a well-developed *claim-God's-riches* prayer habit look like in a believer's life today?

Summing Up
It would be easy to sum up the above verses by focusing on what we get—riches—or how we get them—asking—and to miss the focus on who does the giving: God. Our claiming and receiving riches depends entirely on the giver. Look again at the verses and notice that it is God whom we are approaching, God who gives good gifts, God who gives wisdom, and the Son of God who urges us to "ask...seek...knock." It's because he is wise, powerful, and always present with us that we can make this claim at all.

But why does God require that we ask? The answer is this: God is a person with whom we have a deep and abiding love relationship. He is not an impersonal vending machine, simply a source for what we want or need. The personal asking and the personal giving flows out of and builds on this unique and wonderful Father-child relationship.

Asking and receiving within a relationship cultivates gratitude. You *don't* say thank you to a vending machine. You *do* say thank you to a generous person. Asking also acknowledges dependence. To have to ask is to know that you are weak and he is mighty. Having to ask fosters humility and pulls the rug out from under all pride. At the end of a day in which you have asked for and received spiritual riches, you are driven to humbly give God the credit for every good thing in your life.

Move forward, then, in this session to answer this question: "How can I so fix in my life the habit of claiming God's riches that I will be building my life on his grace, his strength and his wisdom; and cultivating gratitude, dependence and humility?"

Four Steps to Develop the Habit of *Claiming God's Riches*

1. Set the Stage for *Claiming God's Riches.*
- Listen to what God is saying to you in 1 John 5:14-15. Tell him how you respond to its message. Mark key words or thoughts. Prepare to memorize it and to bring it to your petitionary prayer time.
  "This is the confidence we have in approaching God: that if we [continue to] *ask* [for ourselves] *anything according to his will, he hears* [agrees to grant] *us. And if we know that he hears us—whatever we ask—we know that we have what we asked of him."* [Inserts from the meaning of the Greek.]
- Mark those *fruit of the Spirit* from Gal. 5:22-23 that you most want and need:
  love__, joy__, peace__, patience__, kindness__, goodness__, faithfulness__, gentleness__, self-control__.
- Mark the spiritual "*additives*" from 2 Pet. 1:5-8 that you most want and need: faith__, knowledge__, perseverance__, godliness__, brotherly kindness__.

2. Detect Habits That May Hinder *Claiming God's Riches.*
Mark any of the following habits that may be keeping you from *claiming God's riches*:
__ I am not in the habit of asking for spiritual riches and, thus, haven't received much (James 4:2).
__ I don't always ask with complete confidence (faith) that God will deliver (James 1:5).
__ I don't ask with an obedient spirit: "doing what pleases God." (1 Jn. 3:22-23).
__ Most of my prayers have been for temporal blessings rather than spiritual riches.
__ I assume that God is just going to give me his riches without my asking.

3. Launch the *Claiming God's Riches* Habit with a Prayer.
- ♦ *Thank* God for the riches he promises to give. Tell him that you really want and need his good gifts.
- ♦ *Repent* of any sinful habits that have hindered your regularly asking for God's spiritual riches.
- ♦ *Ask* for the specific riches that you have identified above. Trust that God can and will keep his promise to give you what you ask (1 Jn. 5:14-15). Imagine what his answers will look like.
- ♦ *Commit* yourself to regularly ask for "things in accord with his will" and to "obey his commands and do what pleases him" (1 Jn. 3:22).

4. Lock in *Claiming God's Riches* as a Lifetime Habit.
⇒ Continue in the *claiming-God's-riches* habit by repeating the thanking, repenting, asking, and committing steps from the "launch" step above.
⇒ Add to your spiritual riches list as God brings more of his "good gifts" to your attention.
⇒ Watch for God's answers and give him credit for the answers when they come. His answers may come in expected or unexpected ways.

Group Prayer and Covenant Time

The Entire Group Prepares for and Prays Personal Prayers of Confession and Petition.
- Each person selects one **hindering habit**—one you marked in step 2 above—to bring to the whole group prayer time.
- Group members **take one minute** to consider the negative effects of that hindrance and reflect on (or write down) what positive change to ask God for:

_____

_____

- Each person contributes a **two-sentence prayer**: one sentence to confess the hindering habit, and a second sentence to claim God's grace to develop a "right" habit. (Leaders go first.)

The Whole Group Covenants Together Aloud and in Unison

"In utter dependence upon Jesus Christ as my ever-living Savior, Teacher, Lord and prayer partner, I will regularly practice the prayer habit of claiming God's riches and will prayerfully support the others in our Seven Habits group in their pursuit of effective prayer habits."

Small Group Share and Prayer Time
(The session ends when you have finished this prayer time.)

- Each person writes down:
A prayer request for the help you may need to develop the habit of *claiming God's riches*:

  _____
  _____

  Another prayer request for yourself or for one other person:

  _____
  _____

- Each person shares, in two or three sentences, the above two prayer requests with their small group of 2-4 persons.

- Each person prays for one other person in the group, covering the two requests just shared.

AFTER SESSION TWO

Pray for Each Other
Pray for the members of your group, especially your small group, every day with the understanding that things will happen in their prayer lives if you pray for them that won't happen if you don't pray.

Pray about Your Prayer Life
Review key Scripture passages from session two. Pray about your own *claim-God's-riches* prayer habits. Practice this habit daily. Watch carefully for God's leadings. Are there specific "riches" he is leading you to claim? Are there "riches" you are receiving because you have asked?

Develop the Habit of Claiming God's Riches

◊ Ask for one of God's rich gifts using the following three-fold pattern: Ask for it in faith; imagine receiving the gift; thank God for the gift even before you receive it.

◊ Start every day asking for the gift of the Holy Spirit, basing your confidence on Jesus' promise in Luke 11:13. Remember that all God's spiritual blessings are delivered by the Holy Spirit.

◊ Memorize Bible passages that list spiritual blessings or promises, such as Num. 6:24-25, 2 Cor. 13:14, Gal. 5:22-23, and Eph. 6:14-18, and regularly ask God for these.

SESSION 3

Habit Two: **Give God Glory**

To give God glory is to give him what he deserves. He deserves to be praised for who he is. He deserves to be thanked for what he does. He has shown himself to us so that we may acknowledge his greatness, his goodness and his glory. Nothing so deepens our awareness of his power and presence as constant praise. Few things bring greater joy to the heart of God than love-birthed praise. No wonder the Bible is packed with summons for us to glorify God. It challenges us to honor, worship, extol, exalt, laud, magnify, hallow, adore, revere, thank and worship God above all. That's the first and most important way to give him his rightful first place in our lives.

Glorifying God does more than honor God. It also has great personal benefit for us. To give God glory is to take delight in him as we express our love and adoration to him. Praise gladdens our hearts, beautifies our souls and promotes personal holiness. Our sinful inclination toward self-centeredness is reversed when we glorify God and put him at the center of our lives. Our sense of pride in our accomplishments is diminished and humility encouraged when we give God the credit that he deserves. Praising God disrupts the power of evil that circles around us by revealing within us the truth that makes us free, strengthening our faith, and bringing on a new boldness.

Praising God is not something that we do just when we are assembled for public worship. It is meant to be part of our daily lives, to permeate our lives morning, noon and night: "from the rising to the setting sun" (Ps. 113:3). The God-focused psalmist made it his intent to "praise the Lord all my life" (Ps. 146:2). The writer to the Hebrews summons us, through Jesus, to "continually offer to God a sacrifice of praise—the fruit of lips that openly profess his name" (Heb. 13:15). Praising God happens whenever our hearts fill with awe, with reverence, and with gratitude to God, overflowing to give him the glory that he deserves.

Let the following Bible passages focus your attention on God and stretch your prayer life. Let them help you see that giving God glory is the beginning and end of true prayer. Let them help you glorify God all the time, for everything, and with your whole heart. The better you know God, the more you will praise him. The more you praise him, the more you will be blessed. The more you are blessed, the more you will praise him. It's a glorious cycle. Let the praising begin! Let the cycle roll on.

Bible Study for "Give God Glory"

Note that all italics below were inserted by the author of this study.

God Worthy of Praise and Thanks

Shout for joy to the LORD, all the earth. Worship the LORD with gladness; come before him with joyful songs. Know that the LORD is God. It is he who made us, and we are his; we are his people, the sheep of his pasture. Enter his gates with thanksgiving and his courts with praise; give thanks to him and praise his name. For the LORD is good and his love endures forever; his faithfulness continues through all generations. –Ps. 100:1-5

In a loud voice they were saying: "Worthy is the Lamb, who was slain, to receive power and wealth and wisdom and strength and honor and glory and praise!" Then I heard every creature in heaven and on earth and under the earth and on the sea, and all that is in them, saying: "To him who sits on the throne and to the Lamb be praise and honor and glory and power, for ever and ever!" The four living creatures said, "Amen," and the elders fell down and worshiped. –Rev. 5:12-14

Discover

- What different ways does Psalm 100 give us to express praise and thanks to the Lord?

- What six *reasons* does this psalm give us for praising God?

Reflect

- What impresses you most about the worship depicted in these two passages?

- Why would the Lamb of God be worthy of so much praise, by so many, for so long (Rev. 5:12-14)?

Apply

- What would it take to bring modern-day Christians to the level of worship expressed in these verses?

- When and where have you found praise welling up in your heart? What was that like?

- What would the practical difference be in your life if you spent more time praising and thanking God?

God Praised at All Times, in Every Place

Because your love is better than life, my lips will glorify you. I will praise you *as long as I live*, and in your name I will lift up my hands. I will be fully satisfied as with the richest of foods; with singing lips my mouth will praise you.
–Ps. 63:3-5

Praise the LORD. Praise the LORD, you his servants; praise the name of the LORD. Let the name of the LORD be praised, both *now and forevermore*. From the rising of the sun to the place where it sets, the name of the LORD is to be praised. –Ps. 113:1-3

Praise the Lord. Praise the LORD, my soul. I will praise the LORD *all my life*; I will sing praise to my God *as long as I live*. –Ps. 146:1-2

Through Jesus, therefore, let us *continually* offer to God a sacrifice of praise—the fruit of lips that openly profess his name.
–Heb. 13:15

Discover
- What do these verses tell us about the when, where, who, and how of praising God?

Reflect
- What does David mean by saying to God, "Your love is better than life" (Ps.63:1)?

- Why does God deserve to be praised at all times and in all places?

- What does Jesus have to do with the praise we offer to God (Heb. 13:15)?

Apply
- What would make a person want to praise God all the time?

- What would a person's life be like if he or she had the habit of praising God all the time?

God Praised Wholeheartedly

I will give thanks to you, LORD, with *all my heart*; I will tell of all your wonderful deeds. I will be glad and rejoice in you; I will sing the praises of your name, O Most High.   –Ps. 9:1-2

Praise the LORD, my soul; *all my inmost being*, praise his holy name. Praise the Lord, my soul, and forget not all his benefits— who forgives all you sins and heals all your diseases, who redeems your life from the pit and crowns you with love and compassion, who satisfies your desires with good things so that your youth is renewed like the eagle's.   –Ps.103:1-5

I will praise you, LORD, with *all my heart*; before the "gods" I will sing your praise. I will bow down toward your holy temple and will praise your name for your unfailing love and your faithfulness, for you have so exalted your solemn decree that it surpasses your fame.
–Ps. 138:1-2

Discover
- What was it about God that caused the psalmist to give him wholehearted praise?

Reflect
- What does it mean to praise God wholeheartedly? What would characterize half-hearted praise?

- What happens in a person who is giving wholehearted praise to God? What are the outward evidences of wholehearted praise?

Apply
- What wonderful deeds has God done in your life that make you want to sing his praises?

- What things in life can cause you to forget God's benefits and neglect wholehearted praise?

Notable Examples

David praised the LORD in the presence of the whole assembly, saying: "Praise be to you, LORD, the God of our father Israel, from everlasting to everlasting. Yours, LORD, is the greatness and the power and the glory and the majesty and the splendor, for everything in heaven and earth is yours. Yours, LORD, is the kingdom; you are exalted as head over all. Wealth and honor come from you; you are the ruler of all things. In your hands are strength and power to exalt and give strength to all. Now, our God, we give you thanks, and praise your glorious name."   –1 Chron. 29:10-13

(Paul) Oh, the depth of the riches of the wisdom and knowledge of God! How unsearchable his judgments, and his paths beyond tracing out! "Who has known the mind of the Lord? Or who has been his counselor? Who has ever given to God, that God should repay them?" For from him and through him and for him are all things. To him be the glory forever! –Rom. 11:33-36

Discover
- Why, according to David, does God deserve to be praised? (1 Chr. 29:10-13)

- What traits of God does Paul celebrate here?

Reflect
- What's the answer to the three questions that Paul asks in Rom. 11:34-35? What point is he making?

- How, if at all, can we distinguish things are *from* God, things that are *through* God, and things that are *for* God?

Apply
- How can we personally rouse ourselves to more and better praise?

- How can the church rouse itself to greater praise?

Bottom Line Questions
1. What is the single most important idea you are taking away from this *give-God-glory* study?

2. What, practically, might a well-developed *give-God-glory* prayer habit look like in a believer's life today?

Summing Up

"Giving God glory" is a habit of prayer that every believer needs to cultivate. But it is much more than a habit. It grows out of a vision. It is a response to who God is—the God whom you know and love and trust. You can't develop this habit by accumulating praise words or memorizing praise passages. It is not a skill to be cultivated. It's a habit to be developed, not by paying attention to the skill, but by paying attention to God. It must flow out of an awareness of God himself. Alexander Whyte described praise as the ability to "think magnificently about God." If you truly know God and what he has done for you, you will think magnificently about him. If you think magnificently about God, you will give him glory.

The great men of God who gave us the above Scriptures—Paul, John, David and other psalmists—were men who knew their God, men who caught glimpses of his glory. Their expressions of praise and gratitude came from deep within, out of their wholehearted devotion to God. Our pathways to praise will be similar. Don't even try to utter a word of praise until it comes out of your awareness of who God is and what he has done in your life. Think about things like the Father's great love, the Son's gracious redemption, and the Spirit's constant, comforting presence. Then, as you begin to think magnificent thoughts about God, let your prayers of praise and gratitude flow out of that awareness.

Four Steps to Develop the Habit of *Giving God Glory*

1. Set the Stage for *Giving God Glory*

- Turn Romans 11:33-36 into a personal statement of praise to God. Mark in it key words and thoughts that will help you make it your own. Prepare to memorize it so that you can bring it to your *giving-God-glory* prayer time.

    Oh, the depth of the riches of the wisdom and knowledge of God! How unsearchable his judgments, and his paths beyond tracing out! "Who has known the mind of the Lord? Or who has been his counselor? Who has ever given to God, that God should repay them?" For from him and through him and for him are all things. To him be the glory forever!
    – Rom. 11:33-36

- Mark the attributes or activities of the Father, Son, and Holy Spirit below that mean the most to you:
  Father:
  Fatherly goodness__, creator__, sovereign__, almighty__, merciful__, all- wise__, all-knowing__, unchanging__, infinite__, holy__, provides__, righteous__, hates sin (wrath)__.
  Son:
  shows us the Father__, died for us__, raised for us__, is King__, the Way__, the Truth__, the Life__, Light of the world__, Shepherd__, the Word__, abides in us__, will come again__.
  Holy Spirit:
  purifies us__, gives new life__, bears fruit in us__, gives spiritual gifts__, guides us to truth__, gives us faith__, empowers us__, always with us__.

2. Detect Habits That May Hinder *Giving God Glory.*
Mark any of the following habits that may be hindering your *giving God glory:*

___ I am in the habit of verbalizing pat praise phrases without much thought.

___ My eyes have not been as open as they could have been to God's revelation of himself in nature (Rom.1:20).

___ I am just not very conscious of God throughout the hours of the day.

___ I tend to thank God for immediate things, but not much for the many blessings of the past.

3. Launch the *Give God Glory* Habit with a Prayer.
- *Thank* God that he has made himself known to you so that you can knowingly praise and thank him. Thank him for the enrichment of praise and thanksgiving.
- *Repent* of any hindering habits that may be causing you to fail to give God glory.
- *Glorify* God for attributes and activities that you have marked in step 1 above.
- *Ask* God to give you such an awareness of who he is, what he has done, and what he is doing in your life that your heart will be full of praise and gratitude.
- *Commit* yourself to the habit of giving God glory.

4. Lock In *Giving God Glory* as a Lifetime Habit.
⇒ Ask God to open your eyes to his presence and activity in the world at the beginning of each day.

⇒ Regularly repeat the *thank-repent-glorify-ask-commit* steps from the launch step above.

⇒ Expand the praise and gratitude segment of your regularly daily prayers.

⇒ Read the Bible with an eye to what God is doing and an ear to what he is saying to you about himself and his activity in your behalf. Let these insights birth prayers of praise and thanksgiving.

Group Prayer and Covenant Time

The Entire Group Prepares for and Prays Personal Prayers of Confession and Petition

- Each person selects one **hindering habit**—one you marked in step 2 above—to bring to the whole group prayer time.
- Group members **take one minute** to consider the negative effects of that hindrance and reflect on (or write down) what positive change to ask God for:

_____

_____

- Each person contributes a **two-sentence prayer**: one sentence to confess the hindering habit, and a second sentence to claim God's grace to develop a "right" habit. (Leaders go first.)

The Whole Group Covenants Together Aloud and in Unison

"In utter dependence upon Jesus Christ as my ever-living Savior, Teacher, Lord and prayer partner, I will regularly practice the prayer habit of giving God glory and will prayerfully support the others in our Seven Habits group in their pursuit of effective prayer habits."

Small Group Share and Prayer Time
(The session ends with this exercise.)

♦ Each person writes down:
A prayer request for the help you need to develop the habit of ***giving God glory***:

_____

_____

Another prayer request for yourself or for one other person:

_____

_____

♦ Each person shares, in two or three sentences, the above two prayer requests with their small group of 2-4 persons.

♦ Each person prays for one other person in the group, covering the two requests just shared.

AFTER SESSION THREE

Pray for Each Other
Pray for the members of your group, especially your small group, every day with the understanding that things will happen in their prayer lives if you pray for them that won't happen if you don't pray.

Pray about Your Prayer Life
Review key Scripture passages from session three. Pray about your own *give-God-glory* prayer habit. Practice this habit daily. Watch carefully for God's leadings. Are there new ways he is leading you to pray? Are there blessings you are experiencing because you are praising and thanking God more?

Develop the Habit of Giving God Glory

◊ Regularly *ask* God to give you a praising heart and to open your eyes to his greatness and glory so that you may praise him for what you see and know.

◊ Memorize and regularly say praise passages aloud, submitting them to God as your own.

◊ Focus briefly on the unique role each person of the Trinity has in your life. Praise each of the persons—Father, Son and Holy Spirit—for what they mean to you personally.

◊ Read and meditate on one psalm every day. Step into the psalmist's view of God and praise God in line with the praises of the psalmist or in a way that is unique and immediate to you.

◊ Remember and bless God for his *benefits to you*. Recall his blessings, one grouping at a time, using categories such as individuals, groups, special days, spiritual blessings, material blessings, and so on.

SESSION 4

Habit Three: **Seek God's Face**

To seek God's face is to spend one-on-One time with God. It's a time for purposeful aloneness in which we give God our full attention. The primary purpose of alone time with God is intimacy. It's a time to love and be loved; a time to enjoy and be enjoyed by the most important person in our lives. It's not a time to tell God our needs, to intercede for needy friends, or to review grand-scale themes. It's a time to give and receive "I" messages: you speaking to God the Father, Son or Spirit, and any one of the Trinity speaking directly to you.

Jesus envisioned intimacy with God as solitude—closed-door time with the Father. He said, "When you pray, go into your room, close the door and pray to your Father, who is unseen" (Matt. 6:6). Closed-door time with God is better than anything earth has to offer (Ps. 73:25), something our souls thirst for (Ps. 42:1-2), and yearn for (Isa. 26:9). Isaiah assured us that those who stay their minds on God find "perfect peace" (Isa. 26:3), and David discovered that if he kept his eyes always on the Lord, he would be filled with joy in God's presence (Ps.16:8, 11). Jesus himself was the perfect model of seeking the Father's face in solitude (Mk. 1:35; 6:46; Luke 5:15-16; 6:12).

In a way, seeking God's face is easy. God is more eager to have intimate time with us than we could ever imagine. He is knocking at the door of our lives and wanting to come in to commune with us. He asks us to "be still" (Ps. 46:10) and promises to come near to those who call on him and come near to him (Ps. 145:18, Jas. 4:8).

In another way, however, seeking God's face is not so easy. Being quiet and alone with God requires serious discipline in the midst of our busy, strident world. It requires both time and attention. There are no shortcuts. But it is a choice that we can make, and a choice that we have to make if we want to carve out times of deep and meaningful fellowship with him.

Few things in life are more precious than time alone with a good friend. Nothing in life is more precious than time alone with our best friend—God. Ponder the importance of face-to-face time with God as you reflect on the following verses. Walk with the Bible characters who thirsted and longed for fellowship with God. Above all, take time to delight in God and to enjoy precious time with the most important person in your life.

Bible Study for "Seek God's Face"

Note that all italics below were inserted by the author of this study.

God's Presence Sought

One thing I ask from the LORD, this only do I seek: that I may dwell in the house of the LORD all the days of my life, to *gaze on the beauty* of the LORD and to seek him in his temple. . . My heart says of you, "Seek his face." Your face, LORD, *I will seek*." –Ps. 27:4, 8

As the deer pants for streams of water, so my *soul pants* for you, my God. My *soul thirsts* for God, for the living God. When can I go and meet with God? –Ps. 42:1-2

You, God, are my God, earnestly I seek you; I thirst for you, my whole *being longs* for you, in a dry and parched land where there is no water. –Ps. 63:1

Whom have I in heaven but you? And earth has nothing *I desire* besides you. –Ps. 73:25

My *soul yearns* for you in the night; in the morning my spirit longs for you. –Isa. 26:9

Discover
- What words in these verses reveal the writers' deep feelings toward God?

- How many times in these verses do the writers use the pronoun "you" in addressing God? What does that tell you?

Reflect
- What makes God's presence so desirable?

- How can a desire for intimacy with God be cultivated?

- What does it mean for you to seek and meet the Father? The Son of God? The Holy Spirit?

Apply
- Describe, if you can, instances when you yearned for God, when you met God, or when you felt far from God.

- What effect will an increasingly intimate relationship with God have on your prayer life?

God's Presence Found

"*Be still*, and know that I am God; I will be exalted among the nations, I will be exalted in the earth." –Ps. 46:10

The LORD is near to all who *call on* him, to all who call on him in truth. –Ps. 145:18

"But when you pray, go into your room, *close the door* and pray to your Father, who is unseen. Then your Father, who sees what is done in secret, will reward you." –Matt. 6:6

Come near to God and he will come near to you. Wash your hands, you sinners, and purify your hearts, you double-minded. –James 4:8

Mary....sat *at the Lord's feet listening* to what he said. But Martha was distracted by all the preparations that had to be made. She came to him and asked, "Lord, don't you care that my sister has left me to do the work by myself? Tell her to help me!" "Martha, Martha," the Lord answered, "you are worried and upset about many things, but few things are needed—or indeed only one. Mary has chosen what is better, and it will not be taken away from her."—Luke 10:39-42

Discover
- What spiritual habits, according to these verses, will bring a person into the presence of God?

- What was the one thing needful that Mary chose? Why didn't Martha make that choice?

Reflect
- What, practically, does it take for a person to "be still" before God?

- What reward do you suppose the Father has in mind for those who seek him behind closed doors?

- Why would it be necessary to "wash your hands" and "purify your hearts" in order to come near God?

Apply
- Can you share of a time when you made a "Martha" choice? A "Mary" choice?

- When, in the past seven days, did you feel closest to God?

- What difference will it make in your spiritual life if you regularly spend time in God's presence?

God's Presence a Blessing

I keep my eyes always on the LORD. With him at my right hand, I will not be shaken. . . . You make known to me the path of life; you will *fill me with joy* in your presence, with *eternal pleasures* at your right hand. –Ps. 16:8, 11

You keep him in *perfect peace* whose mind is stayed on you, because he trusts in you. –Isa. 26:3 (ESV)

"For where two or three come together in my name, there am *I with* them." –Matt. 18:20

"Here I am! I stand at the door and knock. If anyone hears my voice and opens the door, I will come in and *eat with* that person, and they with me." –Rev. 3:20

Discover
- What spiritual blessings are associated with the presence of God in these verses?

- What do believers have to *do* in order to obtain these blessings?

Reflect
- Why does the presence of God yield the rich spiritual blessings mentioned in these verses?

- Try to describe in your own words what it would be like to be "filled with joy," to have "eternal pleasures," or to have "perfect peace."

- Why is Jesus knocking at the door of our lives?

Apply
- What, if anything, do you need to do that you are not now doing, in order to have more face-to-face time with Jesus?

Notable Examples

The Lord would speak to Moses face to face, as one speaks to a friend. Then Moses would return to the camp, but his young aide Joshua son of Nun did not leave the tent. –Ex. 33:11

"...my servant Moses; he is faithful in all my house. With him I speak face to face, clearly and not in riddles; he sees the form of the LORD."–Num. 12:7-8

Discover

- **What** phrase in Exodus 33:11 describes what it means to speak with God face to face?

Reflect

- What do the descriptions of meeting God "face to face" in these two passages teach us about the nature of a face-to-face relationship with God?

- Jesus says to his disciples in John 15:15: "I have called you friends, for everything that I learned from my Father I have made known to you." What is the link between these words of Jesus and the experience of Moses?

Apply

- What does it mean to have God as a friend?

- What features of a friendship with God are the most appealing to you?

Bottom Line Questions

1. What is the single most important idea you are taking away from this *seek God's face* study?

2. What, practically, might a well-developed *seek God's face* prayer habit look like in a believer's life today?

Summing Up

By meditating on the above verses you stepped into the most splendid studio in the world—the place where you saw firsthand the magnificence of the good and beautiful God. But it was more than a view; it was a meeting with a living person, a person who wanted to spend time with you, to be near you, to hear your voice, and to eat with you.

And he invited you not just to gaze on his beauty. That would have been enough. But Jesus invited you to sit at his feet and learn from him as Mary did. He took you with him into a desolate place to spend time with the Father.

And if you heard his voice and opened the door, he came in and spent time with you over a banquet of love. He filled you with joy, gave you eternal pleasures, and perfected your peace. You spent time with the most important person in your life. And that is what he wants for you, day after day after day.

Four Steps to Develop the Habit of *Seeking God's Face*

1. Set the Stage for *Seeking God's Face.*
- Tell God what he means to you by personalizing Psalm 16:11. Underline key words. Repeat it several times to begin lodging it in your memory.

    You make known to me the path of life; you will fill me with joy in your presence, with eternal pleasures at your right hand. –Ps. 16:11

- To seek God's face is to actively choose be *with* him and to be conscious that he is *with* you. Mark the biblical action steps below that will best help you to seek God's face.
    - ___ I will keep God in mind. ["I have *set the Lord always before* me. Be cause he is at my right hand, I will not be shaken." –Ps. 16:8]
    - ___ I will seek God's face. ["My heart says of you, '*Seek his face*!' Your face Lord, I will seek." –Ps. 27:8]
    - ___ I will call on the Lord. ["The Lord is near to all who *call on him*, to all who call on him in truth." –Ps. 145:18]
    - ___ I will get as close to God as possible. ["*Come near to G*od and he will come near to you." –Jas. 4:8]
    - ___ I will invite Christ into my life for a time of fellowship. ["I stand at the door and knock. If anyone hears my voice and *opens the door*, I will come in and eat with him, and he with me." –Rev. 3:20]

2. Detect Habits That May Hinder *Seeking God's Face.*
Which of the following habits may hinder your having **face-to-face** time with God?
- ___ I am so busy that I don't often take time to *seek God's face.*
- ___ I spend most of my prayer time asking God to fix things in my life or the lives of others.
- ___ I haven't come to the point of really enjoying intimacy with God.
- ___ I just don't know how to have a meaningful face-to-face meeting with God—an invisible, spiritual person.
- ___ I know I am a sinner, and I just don't feel comfortable in God's presence.

3. Launch the *Seek God's Face* Habit with a Prayer.

- *Thank* God for the incredible privilege of having a person-to-person love relationship with him.
- *Repent* of any hindering habit that may keeping you from *seeking God's face*.
- *Ask* God to help you overcome any hesitation in meeting him and to appreciate the unspeakable joy of a *face-to-face* experience with him. Invite him to reveal himself to you.
- *Commit* to one-on-one time with the Father, Son or Holy Spirit. Keep your verbal exchange with God in person-to-person, I/you language -- you speaking to God and he to you.

4. Lock in *Seeking God's Face* as a Lifetime Habit.

⇒ Set a definite time to meet God one-on-one each day. Focus your attention on him and enjoy his company. Use some of the biblical descripttions of closeness to God listed above.

⇒ Repeat the *thank-repent-ask-commit* pattern from step 3 above as often as necessary.

⇒ End each *face-to-face* time with God by asking him to break through to you again and again throughout each day.

Group Prayer and Covenant Time

The Entire Group Prepares for and Prays Personal Prayers of Confession and Petition

- Each person selects one **hindering habit**—one you marked in step 2 above—to bring to the whole group prayer time.
- Group members **take one minute** to consider the negative effects of that hindrance and reflect on (or write down) what positive change to ask God for:

_____

_____

- Each person contributes a **two-sentence prayer**: one sentence to confess the hindering habit, and a second sentence to claim God's grace to develop a "right" habit. (Leaders go first.)

The Whole Group Covenants Together Aloud and in Unison

"In utter dependence upon Jesus Christ as my ever-living Savior, Teacher, Lord and prayer partner, I will regularly practice the prayer habit of seeking God's face and will prayerfully support the others in our Seven Habits group in their pursuit of effective prayer habits."

Small Group Share and Prayer Time
(The session ends with this exercise.)

- Each person writes down:
  A prayer request for the help you need to develop the habit of **seeking God's face**:

  _____

  _____

  Another prayer request for yourself or for one other person:

  _____

  _____

- Each person shares, in two or three sentences, the above two prayer requests with their small group of 2-4 persons.

- Each person prays for one other person in the group covering the two requests just shared.

AFTER SESSION FOUR

Pray for Others
Pray for the members of your small group every day, with the understanding that things will happen in their prayer lives if you pray for them that won't happen if you don't pray.

Pray about Your Prayer Life
Review key Scripture passages from session four. Pray about your own *seek-God's-face* prayer habit. Practice this habit daily. Watch carefully for God's leadings. What is God saying to you in these face-to-face times? What are you saying to him?

Develop the Habit of Seeking God's Face

- ◊ *Ask* God to quiet your heart and help you to focus solely on him. Invite him to personally reveal himself to you.

- ◊ Relax your body, and quiet mind and emotions as completely as possible. Don't use this time to do plan, write, or ask for stuff. Just *be* in his presence.

- ◊ Think of God in personal terms. Remember that he is a thinking, acting, willing, feeling, talking, listening person who is *with* you.

- ◊ *Keep a one-on-One focus.* Meditate on what he thinks of you, has done for you, is doing for you, has promised you, or expects of you. Share your thoughts with him. Tell him how much he means to you, why you love him, that you trust him, how you are serving him and how much you need him. Give him 50 percent or more of the talk time.

- ◊ Ask God what he wants to say to you right now that will meet the needs of your heart. Then pause and listen. Invite him to identify sins in your life that you may not be aware of.

- ◊ Respond to what God says to you and invite him to respond to what you say to him, as in a normal conversation.

SESSION 5

Habit Four: **Win over Sin**

Sin, according to the Bible, is missing the mark of God's standard for our lives. That sounds like simply breaking a law. But it's worse than that. It's breaking a relationship with the most important person in our lives: God. It's rebelling against God, distrusting his promises and spurning his love. Some sins are flagrant actions, like sexual immorality, murder, theft or drunkenness. However, more common—especially among believers—are subtle sins like pride, lust, envy, slander, deceit and selfish ambition. Whether flagrant or subtle, all sin is equally displeasing to God. All needs to be dealt with lest it lead to ruin and destruction.

Sin has tragic consequences, especially when it comes to our relationship with God. It separates us from God, hinders prayer and robs us of the pleasure of his presence. It deprives us of God-intended blessings and sows the seeds of anxiety, fear, loneliness, failure and despair. If not dealt with, sin has the power to cause suffering, spiritual blindness, hardness of heart, guilt, and shame; it leads inevitably to God's judgment. Sin is our biggest problem. Sin has been the undoing of the human race.

But there is hope—hope for overcoming both the *guilt* and the *impurity* of sin. Overcoming starts with confession. John said it most clearly: "If we confess our sins, he [God] is faithful and just and will forgive our sins and purify us from all unrighteousness" (1 Jn. 1:9). Overcoming continues with repentance—turning away from sin and returning to our love relationship with God.

There is also hope for overcoming the *power* of sin - that lethal force that operates through the world, the flesh and the devil and constantly seeks to goad us into sinful actions. By means of our crucifixion with Christ we have victory over the flesh and we are "no longer slaves to sin" (Rom. 6:6). Through our faith in Christ we have victory over the world (1 John 5:4-5). And because the Son of God appeared to destroy the devil's work, we are delivered from him (Matt. 6:13).

Study the ensuing Scripture passages with an awareness of the terribleness of sin. Judith Viorst entitled her notable children's book *Alexander and the Terrible, Horrible, No Good, Very Bad Day*. Let me say, echoing her title, that sin is a terrible, horrible, no good, very bad thing. It is terrible not only because it may lead to eternal destruction, but also because it can lead to daily devastation, even in the life of a believer.

Work through these verses with an awareness that God hates sin and opposes every shape and form it may take. Learn how, like God, you can oppose sin whenever and wherever it may touch your life. Learn how to use prayer effectively in overcoming sin. You *can* win over sin! You *can* live a victorious Christian life!

Bible Study for "Win over Sin"

Note that all italics below were inserted by the author of this study.

Set Free from the Guilt of Sin

Whoever conceals their sins does not prosper, but the one who confesses and renounces them *finds mercy*. –Pr. 28:13

Let the wicked forsake their ways and the unrighteous their thoughts. Let them turn to the LORD, and he will *have mercy* on them, and to our God, for he will *freely pardon*. –Isa. 55:7

If we confess our sins, he is faithful and just and *will forgive* us our sins and *purify* us from all unrighteousness. –1 Jn. 1:9

Who is a God like you, who *pardons* sin and *forgives* the transgression of the remnant of his inheritance? You do not stay angry forever but delight to *show mercy*. –Micah 7:18

He himself [Christ] *bore our sins*" in his body on the cross, so that we might die to sins and live for righteousness; by his wounds you have been healed. –1 Pet. 2:24

Discover

- What action steps are required before we can expect divine forgiveness?

- What words from these passages describe God's way of dealing with the sin of people who are repentant?

- What did Christ do with our sins? What are the results of what Christ did?

Reflect

- How can we be sure that our sins will not eternally separate us from God?

- Is there a difference between God's pardoning us, forgiving us, or purifying us?

Apply

- What will you do to stay free from the guilt of sin?

Set Free from the Old Sinful Self

For we know that our *old self was crucified* with him so that the body ruled by sin might be done away with, that we should no longer be slaves to sin—because anyone who has died has been set free from sin. . . . In the same way, *count yourselves dead* to sin but alive to God in Christ Jesus. Therefore do not let sin reign in your mortal body so that you obey its evil desires. –Rom. 6:6-7, 11-12

So I say, walk by the Spirit, and you will *not gratify* the desires of the flesh. For the flesh desires what is contrary to the Spirit, and the Spirit what is contrary to the flesh. They are in conflict with each other, so that you are not to do whatever you want. But if you are led by the Spirit, you are not under the law. –Gal. 5:16-18

For if you live according to the flesh, you will die; but if by the Spirit you *put to death* the misdeeds of the body, you will live. For those who are led by the Spirit of God are the children of God. –Rom. 8:13-14

Discover
- How are we set free from the power of sin? How does that affect the way that we think of ourselves?

- What are the benefits of being free from sin?

Reflect
- What does it mean to "count yourself dead to sin"? Is that the same as "putting to death the misdeeds of the body"?

- What are the desires of the sinful flesh? What are the desires of the Spirit?

- What does it mean to be "alive to God in Christ Jesus"?

Apply
- Why is the Spirit's role critically important in your battle with the flesh?

- What will the Christian life be like if you are led by the Spirit?

Overcoming the World

"Watch and pray so that you will not fall into *temptation*. The spirit is willing, but the flesh is weak." –Matt. 26:41

Do *not love the world* or anything in the world. If anyone loves the world, love for the Father is not in them. For everything in the world -- the lust of the flesh, the lust of the eyes, and the pride of life -- comes not from the Father but from the world. The world and its desires pass away, but whoever does the will of God lives forever. –1 Jn. 2:15-17

For everyone born of God *overcomes* the world. This is the victory that has overcome the world, even our faith. Who is it that overcomes the world? Only the one who believes that Jesus is the Son of God. –1 Jn. 5:4-5

Do not conform to the pattern of this world, but be transformed by the renewing of your mind. Then you will be able to test and approve what God's will is-- his good, pleasing and perfect will. –Rom. 12:2

Discover
- Why is prayer so important when it comes to preventing sin? (Matt. 26:41)

- How should we respond to the "world"? Why? What happens to the world and those who buy into it?

- Who is it that overcomes the world? What is the opposite of being conformed to the world?

Reflect
- What is the world, in the context of these Scriptures? How do you see the world impacting us today?

- What is there about faith that gives believers victory over the world?

Apply
- What is one way that the world is trying to squeeze you into its mold? What are you doing to overcome?

Win over the Devil

"This, then, is how you should pray: ...Lead us not into temptation, but *deliver* us from the *evil one*."– Matt. 6:9, 13

"Simon, Simon, Satan has asked to sift all of you as wheat. But I have prayed for you, Simon, that your faith may not fail. And when you have turned back, strengthen your brothers." –Luke 22:31-32

"The world has hated [my followers], for they are not of the world any more than I [Jesus] am of the world. My prayer is not that you take them out of the world but that you *protect them* from the *evil one*." –John 17:14-15

Submit yourselves, then, to God. Resist the *devil*, and he will flee from you. –Jas. 4:7

The one who does what is sinful is of the devil, because the devil has been sinning from the beginning. The reason the Son of God appeared was to destroy the *devil's work*. –1 John 3:8

Discover
- How, according to Jesus' teaching on prayer, can believers be protected from the evil one?

- How did Jesus' life demonstrate the protective power of prayer?

Reflect
- How important, compared to the other parts of the Lord's Prayer, is the last phrase—"deliver us from the evil one"?

- List several different ways that the devil's work is thwarted by Jesus' coming to earth.

- What is Jesus doing right now to defeat the devil? What will he do in the future?

Apply
- What will you do to defeat the devil in days ahead? What are your chances of success?

- Do you tend to under- or overestimate the devil's influence in our world?

Bottom Line Questions

1. What is the single most important idea you are taking away from this *win over sin* study?

2. What, practically, might a well-developed *win over sin* prayer habit look like in a believer's life today?

Summing Up

Everybody wants to win. Children want to win their games. Baseball players want to win the World Series. Football teams are known to give everything to win the Super Bowl. And sports fans count their teams' win as their own.

God wants to win too, and he *has* won. He has won the greatest victory of all—the win over sin. He has won it for us, his children, through the death of his Son on the cross. He invites us to step into that win with him, to claim it as our own. And though he has won, and we have won with him, the game is not over. We continue to do battle with sin every day, and by his grace we are able to win the ongoing battle with sin.

The Son of God is our coach, a coach who both directs us and empowers us by his Spirit to win over sin. And prayer is the action step by which his guidance is secured and his power released to accomplish this incredible win, a win over the world, the flesh and the devil. That win is bigger than the World Series or the Super Bowl. Really! It's the win of a lifetime, an eternal lifetime. You can do it! You can win over sin. So go for it!

Four Steps to Develop the Habit of *Winning over Sin*

1. Set the Stage for *Winning over Sin.*
- Embrace Jesus' challenge in Matthew 26:41. Tell him that you will "watch and pray" in the face of temptation, knowing that your "flesh is weak." Repeat the verse several times in order to begin memorizing it.

    "Watch and pray so that you will not fall into temptation. The spirit is willing, but the flesh is weak." –Matt. 26:41

- *Winning over sin* begins by asking the Holy Spirit to search you and help you identify those sins to which you are most prone. Mark the sins in the following list to which you are most susceptible. These are mostly subtle sins. Any not-so-subtle sins you may have to deal with will be extensions of these:
pride__, anger__, lust__, envy__, worry__, covetousness__, gluttony__, lying__, gossip__, ungentleness__, bitterness__, materialism__, greed__, sloth__, impatience__, hatred__, worldliness__, unforgiving__, unforbearing__, unloving__.

2. Detect Habits that May Hinder *Winning over Sin.*
Which of the following habits may hinder your *winning over sin*?

___ I often pray a general forgive-my-sins prayer but don't usually get very specific.

___ I am more inclined to ask forgiveness for sin after the fact than to get God's grace upfront before I fail.

___ I haven't taken subtle sins very seriously. I am not used to asking the Holy Spirit to help me identify them.

___ I haven't really come to grips with the fact that sin, even subtle sin, has tragic consequences.

___ I haven't tried very hard to win over sin since I know that God has forgiven all my sins and I am certain of getting to heaven.

3. Launch the *Win-Over-Sin* Habit with a Prayer.
- *Thank* God for all he has done to give you a *win over sin:* forgiveness through the cross, new life through Christ's resurrection, cleansing from past sin and Spirit-given victory over future temptation.
- *Repent* of any hindering habit (above) that may keep you from *winning over sin.*
- *Ask* forgiveness for known sin and hidden faults, and for complete cleansing. Ask for the ability, from now on, to crucify the flesh, over come the world and resist Satan.
- *Commit* yourself to victory over the world, the flesh and the devil.

4. Lock in *Winning over Sin* as a Lifetime Habit.
⇒ Memorize and pray Ps. 139:23-24. Continue to ask God's help to identify specific sins.

⇒ Keep a short, easily-remembered list of those areas where you are the most susceptible to sin (see step 1 above). Regularly ask God to help you see why he hates these sins, what harm they cause, and how to dig out their roots. Revise and expand the list as you progress in sanctification.

⇒ Regularly repeat the *thank-repent- ask-commit* steps from step 3 above.

Group Prayer and Covenant Time

The Entire Group Prepares for and Prays Personal Prayers of Confession and Petition

- Each person selects one **hindering habit**—one you marked in step 2 above—to bring to the whole group prayer time.
- Group members **take one minute** to consider the negative effects of that hindrance and reflect on (or write down) what positive change to ask God for:

_____

_____

- Each person contributes a **two-sentence prayer**: one sentence to confess the hindering habit, and a second sentence to claim God's grace to develop a "right" habit. (Leaders go first.)

The Whole Group Covenants Together Aloud and in Unison

"In utter dependence upon Jesus Christ as my ever-living Savior, Teacher, Lord and prayer partner, I will regularly practice the prayer habit of winning over sin and will prayerfully support the others in our Seven Habits group in their pursuit of effective prayer habits."

Small Group Share and Prayer Time
(The session ends with this exercise.)

- Each person writes down:
A prayer request for the help you need to develop the habit of **winning over sin:**

_____

_____

Another prayer request for yourself or for one other person:

_____

_____

- Each person shares, in two or three sentences, the above two prayer requests with their small group of 2-4 persons.

- Each person prays for one other person in the group covering the two requests just shared.

AFTER SESSION FIVE

Pray for Others
Pray for the members of your small group every day, with the understanding that things will happen in their prayer lives if you pray for them that won't happen if you don't pray.

Pray about Your Prayer Life
Review key Scripture passages from session five. Pray about your own *win-over-sin* prayer habit. Practice this habit daily. Watch carefully for God's leadings. Are you finding freedom from guilt for past sins? Are you gaining upfront advantage over the world, the flesh and the devil?

Develop the "Win over Sin" Prayer Habit
◊ Read and meditate on the Word every day and *ask* God to use his Word to reveal and counteract all forms of sin in your life. Ask him also to use the Word in such a way that you are kept from sin (Ps. 119:11) and "thoroughly equipped for every good work" (2 Tim. 3:17).

◊ At the end of every day, *ask* God to reveal to you any sins of thought, word or deed that remain unconfessed. Confess and renounce those sins and ask God's forgiveness. Thank him for forgiving you and purifying your heart.

◊ Be keenly aware of the three diabolical enemies of the Christian life: the world, the flesh, and the devil. Seek God's help to overcome them every day.

◊ Flee from any situation—such as a relationship, Internet site, TV program, movie, or location—that might lead you to compromise your spiritual integrity.

SESSION 6

Habit Five: **Hear God's Voice**

"God is a talker. He has always been a talker. If God had remained silent we would have no way of knowing him at all."[1] God wants us to listen to him so that he can reveal himself to us and guide our lives. Jesus said, "It is written in the Prophets: 'They will all be taught by God.' Everyone who has heard the Father and learned from him comes to me" (Jn. 6:45). The prophet Isaiah, speaking for God, connects listening to spiritual guidance: "Whether you turn to the right or to the left, your ears will hear a voice behind you saying, 'This is the way, walk in it'" (Isa. 30:21). For Jesus, listening was the way for believers to live in an ongoing relationship with him: "My sheep listen to my voice; I know them, and they follow me" (Jn. 10:27).

The primary way we hear God speak to us today is through the Bible. The psalmist writes: "Your word is a lamp for my feet, a light on my path" (Ps. 119:105). It would be foolish for anyone to seek to hear God and neglect the Word of God. But the Spirit, through whom we have received divine revelation, is also able to speak directly to our hearts, as Paul reminds us: "The Spirit himself testifies with our spirit that we are God's children" (Rom. 8:16). Listening to God also means listening to Christ, the Son of God. It is he who stands at the door and knocks, saying, "If anyone hears my voice and opens the door, I will come in and eat with that person, and they with me" (Rev. 3:20).

Jesus himself showed us what it means to listen to the Father. Accepting his complete dependence on the Father, he conceded, "By myself I can do nothing; I judge only as I hear" (Jn. 5:30). A bit later he acknowledged, "My teaching… comes from the one who sent me" (Jn. 7:16; see also 8:28, 12:50). Jesus clearly was a listener. And since we live in him and he in us, we can lean on the Father and learn from him in the same way that Jesus did.

Getting ideas from the Bible is one thing. Meeting the Author, who is alive and well today, is another thing. Read and reflect on the following Scripture passages with a prayer that you will not only gain insights from the Word, but that you will hear God speaking to you personally. Put yourself into the shoes of Isaiah, David, and Paul. Make their words your words. Choose what is best, and sit with Mary at Jesus' feet. Commune with God by putting your name in the place of the personal pronouns in these verses. Be one of the "sheep" who listen to the Shepherd's voice. Hear the knock and the voice of Jesus, who wants to "come in and eat" with you. Learn to live "by every word that comes from the mouth of God."

---

[1] Vander Griend, *The Joy of Prayer*, p. 34.

Bible Study for "Hear God's Voice"

Note that all italics below were inserted by the author of this study.

Hearing God in Scripture

Your word is *a lamp* for my feet, *a light* on my path. –Ps. 119:105

"As the rain and the snow come down from heaven, and do not return to it without watering the earth and making it bud and flourish, so that it yields seed for the sower and bread for the eater, so is *my word that goes out from my mouth*: It will not return to me empty, but will accomplish what I desire and achieve the purpose for which I sent it." –Isa. 55:10-11

"These are the ones I look on with favor: those who are humble and contrite in spirit, and who *tremble at my word*." –Isa. 66:2b

All Scripture is God-breathed and is useful for teaching, rebuking, correcting and training in righteousness, so that the servant of God may be thoroughly equipped for every good work. –2 Tim. 3:16-17

Discover
- How is the Word of God like a lamp, like rain and snow?

- What, according to these verses, are some things that God accomplishes through his Word?

- How do we have to respond to God's Word if it is to be effective in our lives?

Reflect
- What does the phrase "God-breathed" tell us about the origin and purpose of Scripture?

- What would you expect to see in the life of a believer who is "thoroughly equipped for every good work"?

Apply
- What Scripture reading habits have you found to be the most helpful?

- What is one Scripture passage that has deeply affected your life? How did it affect you?

Hearing God for Life

I will *instruct you* and *teach you* in the way you should go; I will counsel you with my loving eye on you. –Ps. 32:8

Trust in the LORD with all your heart and lean not on your own understanding; in all your ways *submit to him*, and he will make your paths straight. –Prov. 3:5-6

This is what the LORD says -- your Redeemer, the Holy One of Israel: "I am the LORD your God, who teaches you what is best for you, who *directs you* in the way you should go. If only you had paid attention to my commands, your peace would have been like a river, your well-being like the waves of the sea." –Isa. 48:17-18

Jesus answered, "It is written: Man shall not live on bread alone, but on *every word* that comes from the mouth of God." –Matt. 4:4

Discover
- What are some ways that God helps those who listen to him?

- What do believers have to do to keep on "the way they should go"? What will it cost them if they don't?

Reflect
- What does it mean to lean on your own understanding? What could be bad about that?

- What would a life lived "by every word that comes from the mouth of God" look like?

Apply
- What patterns of life may keep us from being attentive to God's Word?

- Where have you experienced the leading of the Lord because you listened to him?

Listening to Jesus

Then a cloud appeared and covered them, and a voice came from the cloud: "This is my Son, whom I love. *Listen* to him!" –Mk. 9:7

"I have other sheep that are not of this sheep pen. I must bring them also. They too will *listen* to my voice, and there shall be one flock and one shepherd. . . . My sheep *listen* to my voice; I know them, and they follow me. I give them eternal life, and they shall never perish; no one will snatch them out of my hand." –Jn. 10:16, 27-28

Mary . . . sat at the Lord's feet *listening* to what he said.... "Few things are needed—or indeed only one. Mary has chosen what is better, and it will not be taken away from her." –Luke 10:39, 42

"Here I am! I stand at the door and knock. If anyone *hears* my voice and opens the door, I will come in and eat with that person, and they with me." –Rev. 3:20

Discover
- What are some ways that Jesus' followers are blessed if they listen to his voice?

- What does Jesus promise to those who open the door when he knocks?

Reflect
- What are we going to hear if we listen to the Son of God? How will listening to Jesus affect our lives?

- Is there a way for us to listen to Jesus Mary-style in the midst of our hectic, busy lives?

- If you had dinner with Jesus, what would you most like to talk about with him? What would he most like to talk about with you?

Apply
- When it comes to your relationship with Jesus, do you tend to be a "Mary" or a "Martha"?

- How do you distinguish the voice of Jesus from the many others that vie for your attention?

Hearing the Holy Spirit

"But the Advocate, the Holy Spirit, whom the Father will send in my name, will teach you all things and will *remind* you of everything I have said to you." –Jn. 14:26 (see also Jn. 16:12-15)

The Spirit himself *testifies* with our spirit that we are God's children. –Rom. 8:16

I keep asking that the God of our Lord Jesus Christ, the glorious Father, may give you the Spirit of wisdom and *revelation*, so that you may know him better. –Eph. 1:17

As for you, the anointing you received from him remains in you, and you do not need anyone to teach you. But as his anointing *teaches* you about all things and as that anointing is real, not counterfeit—just as it has *taught* you, remain in him. –1 Jn. 2:27

"Whoever has ears, let them *hear* what the Spirit says to the churches." –Rev. 2:7

Discover
- What do we learn from these verses about the Holy Spirit?

- What are the spiritual benefits of hearing the Spirit testify? What is he teaching us?

Reflect
- What can we do to "hear" what the Spirit is saying to us? What may hinder our hearing the Spirit's voice?

- When the Spirit teaches us "about all things," what is that likely to include?

Apply
- On what topics would you most like to hear from the Spirit?

- Is there a person you know who needs to receive "the Spirit of wisdom and revelation so that they may know him [God] better"? Say a prayer for that person!

Jesus, an Example of Hearing

"By myself I [Jesus] can do nothing; I judge only as *I hear*, and my judgment is just, for I seek not to please myself but him who sent me." –Jn. 5:30

Jesus answered, "My teaching is not my own. It comes from the one who sent me." –Jn. 7:16

So Jesus said, "When you have lifted up the Son of Man, then you will know that I am he and that I do nothing on my own but speak just what *the Father has taught* me." –Jn. 8:28

"I know that his command leads to eternal life. So whatever I say is just what the *Father has told* me to say." –Jn. 12:49-50

Discover
- How did Jesus come to be so wise, and to be such a good teacher?

Reflect
- Why didn't Jesus rely on his own insights to judge and teach?

- What can we learn about listening to the Father from Jesus' example?

Apply
- What difference, if any, has hearing God made in your life?

Bottom Line Questions

1. What is the single most important idea you are taking away from this *hear-God's-voice* study?

2. What, practically, might a well-developed *hear-God's-voice* prayer habit look like in a believer's life today?

Summing Up

When it comes to "hearing," everything depends on who is doing the talking. We have all listened to people talk about things that are boring and unimportant. We've heard speakers who were dull and monotonous. The wonderful thing about being able to hear God is not simply that we have mastered a listening technique, but that it is the all-wise God who is communicating. What he says is of the greatest importance and is positively life-giving. It is instruction on the way we should go, teaching that will keep us from sin, a word that we can live by, truth that will set us free. It is training in righteousness and equipping for every good work.

But God is not just a life-giving talker. He is also a listener. He doesn't simply want to be an advisor who tells us what to believe and what to do. Nor does he want to be just an "ear" who hears and answers our prayers. He wants a relationship—a love relationship. That requires both talking and listening, thoughtful talking and listening. God does that very well—perfectly, in fact. The question that remains for us is, "How well are *we* doing at talking to God and listening to him?" That's really what these sessions are all about.

Four Steps to Develop the Habit of *Hearing God's Voice*

1. Set the Stage for *Hearing God's Voice.*
- Personalize John 10:27 by putting yourself in the place of a sheep *and* hearing what the Shepherd says of you. Memorize the verse and make it your personal testimony.

    "My sheep listen to my voice; I know them, and they follow me."
    –Jn. 10:27

- On which of the following **topics** would you most like to "hear" God's thoughts:
  how to hear his voice__, his direction when I am uncertain__, how to win over a sin__, how to gain humility__, how to relate to a certain person__, how to cope in a difficulty situation__, how to deal with worry__, how to deal with a thorn in the flesh__, how to share the gospel with a friend__, how to use my time__, other: _____.

2. Detect Habits that May Hinder *Hearing God's Voice.*
Which of the following habits may hinder your *hearing God's voice*
___ I haven't meditated on the Word of God "day and night" so that I can "be careful to do everything written in it" (Josh. 1:8; Ps. 1:2).
___ I often make life choices without giving God the chance to speak into my situation (Isa. 30:21).
___ I am sometimes a Martha, "distracted with much serving," rather than a Mary, "who sat at Jesus' feet listening to what he said" (Luke 10:39-40)
___ Though Jesus said, "My sheep hear my voice," I don't listen for his voice (Jn. 10:27).
___ I have not regularly asked the Father to give me "the Spirit of wisdom and *revelation*" so that I might know him better (Eph. 1:18).

3. **Launch the *Hear God's Voice* Habit with a Prayer.**
    - *Thank* God for speaking clearly today through his Word and Spirit.
    - *Repent* of any hindering habit (above) that may keep you from *hearing God's voice*.
    - *Tell* God that you really want to know his will and that you need his help to hear his voice.
    - *Ask* him to give you an ear to hear what he wants you to hear (Jn. 10:27, Rev.2:7). Trust that he is willing and able to help you hear.
    - *Commit* yourself to hearing what God says to you and responding fully and obediently.

4. **Lock in *Hearing God's Voice* as a Lifetime Habit.**
    ⇒ Regularly repeat the *thank-repent-tell-ask-commit* steps from the *hearing-God's-voice* prayer above.
    ⇒ When reading Scripture, always ask God to help you hear what he is saying to you.
    ⇒ Pick a topic on which you would like to hear God speak from the step 1 above. Invite him to speak on that topic in his own time and way. Listen carefully.
    ⇒ If you think you have heard God speak but are still uncertain it was him, ask him to confirm his message in other ways. He really wants you to know what he has said.

Group Prayer and Covenant Time

The Entire Group Prepares for and Prays Personal Prayers of Confession and Petition

- Each person selects one **hindering habit**—one you marked in step 2 above—to bring to the whole group prayer time.
- Group members **take one minute** to consider the negative effects of that hindrance and reflect on (or write down) what positive change to ask God for:

_____

_____

- Each person contributes a **two-sentence prayer**: one sentence to confess the hindering habit, and second sentence to claim God's grace to develop a "right" habit. (Leaders go first.)

The Whole Group Covenants Together Aloud and in Unison

"In utter dependence upon Jesus Christ as my ever-living Savior, Teacher, Lord and prayer partner, I will regularly practice the prayer habit of hearing God's voice and will prayerfully support the others in our Seven Habits group in their pursuit of effective prayer habits."

Small Group Share and Prayer Time
(The session ends with this exercise.)

- Each person writes down:
  A prayer request for the help you need to develop the habit of *hearing God's voice*:

  _____

  _____

  Another prayer request for yourself or for one other person:

  _____

  _____

- Each person shares, in two or three sentences, the above two prayer requests with their small group of 2-4 persons.

- Each person prays for one other person in the group covering the two requests just shared.

AFTER SESSION SIX

Pray for Others
Pray for the members of your small group every day, with the understanding that things will happen in their prayer lives if you pray for them that won't happen if you don't pray.

Pray about Your Prayer Life
Review key Scripture passages from session six. Pray about your own *hear-God's-voice* prayer habit. Practice this habit daily. Watch carefully for God's leadings. Are you hearing better? Are you hearing regularly?

Develop the "Hear God's Voice" Prayer Habit

◊ *Spend time in the Word.* The Bible is God's primary way of speaking to us, so hearing him speak through the Scriptures is the best way to learn to listen. Let him speak to your heart and life as much as to your head. Let him direct you as to when, where, and how to apply the truths you are hearing. That's also part of listening.

◊ *Practice listening.* Use a listening time to place questions, problems and issues before God. "Who do you want me to pray for?" How should I pray for _____?" "What sins do I need to deal with?" "What must I do about _____?" "What do you want to say to me, God?" Then wait on God to direct your thoughts or give you impressions. Test what you think he is saying by the Word. He will never say anything that contradicts his Word.

◊ *Stop* and listen before you pray. *Invite* the Holy Spirit to teach you who and what to pray for. He doesn't usually speak uninvited. Give the Holy Spirit the time and space to guide your prayers.

◊ *Be assured* that, if the Holy Spirit is in you, hearing God is normal. The Word of God says so: "As for you, the anointing you received from him remains in you, and you do not need anyone to teach you.... his anointing teaches you about all things." –1 Jn. 2:27

SESSION 7

Habit Six: **Pray for Family and Friends in Christ**

Intercession is prayer for others. Intercessors stand in between those in need and the One who is able to meet that need. They are like the "friend in the middle" of Jesus' parable in Luke 11:5-8. In this story, a man's friend has come from far away, and the man has nothing offer his hungry guest. So, unable to help his friend in need, the man goes to a friend with bread and boldly pleads for the needed bread. Though initially ignored, he continues to knock and plead until he receives the bread to provide for his guest's need. That "friend in the middle" is, for Jesus, a model of intercession. As intercessors we stand between a needy world and the God whose power and grace can meet those needs. Our role, Jesus is saying, is to keep on knocking at the door of heaven until God's provisions are released.

The Bible is filled with intercessors. Think of Abraham, the man of prayer; Moses, the mighty intercessor; Elijah, the praying prophet; David, the praying king; Ezra, the praying reformer; Nehemiah, the praying builder; Daniel, the praying captive; Anna and Simeon, who prayed for Jesus' coming; and Paul, the praying apostle to the Gentiles. All were powerful intercessors. We can learn a lot about intercession from the lives of these great prayer warriors. Jesus Christ was the greatest of all intercessors. Seven out of his nine recorded prayers were prayers of intercession. Today he continues to make intercession for his people and his kingdom (Heb. 7:25).

Intercession is of prime importance in the ongoing work of God. People around you desperately need your intercessory prayers. Your first responsibility is to pray for those who are closest to you—family and close friends. Beyond that first circle is another for whom God expects you to intercede: your spiritual family—friends of faith and those who serve you in leadership roles in the Christian community. Prayer is vital in these close relationships, because your friends and family need more than you can give them. They need most what God can give, and God gives in response to asking. God has much to give, and he is pleased to bless them with spiritual riches in response to our prayers.

Embrace your role as an intercessor in the family of God as you do the following Bible study. Learn what it means to be an intercessor by observing the way that Job, Jesus, the early church, and the apostle Paul prayed. Learn what God expects of you as an intercessor and what he really wants you to be praying about. See yourself as a servant of God who is authorized to release his power and grace into the lives of your family and friends in Christ.

Bible Study for "Pray for Family and Friends in Christ"

Note that all italics below were inserted by the author of this study.

Praying for Family and Friends

His [Job's] sons used to hold feasts in their homes on their birthdays. . . . When a period of feasting had run its course, Job would make arrangements for them to be purified. Early in the morning he would *sacrifice a burnt offering* for each of them, thinking, "Perhaps my children have sinned and cursed God in their hearts." This was Job's regular custom. –Job. 1: 4-5

Then Jesus said to them, "Suppose you have a friend, and you go to him at midnight and say, 'Friend, lend me three loaves of bread; a friend of mine on a journey has come to me, and I have no food to offer him.' And suppose the one inside answers, 'Don't bother me. The door is already locked, and my children and I are in bed. I can't get up and give you anything.' I tell you, even though he will not get up and give you the bread because of friendship, yet because of your shameless audacity he will surely get up and give you as much as you need."
–Luke 11:5-8

People were bringing little children to Jesus for him to *place his hands on them*, but the disciples rebuked them. . . . And he took the children in his arms, placed his hands on them and *blessed them*. –Mark 10:13,16

Discover

- What moved Job to pray (offer sacrifices) for his children? What does this teach us about praying for family members?

- What do we learn about intercession from Jesus' parable of the midnight friend?

- What does Jesus' prayerful blessing of children teach us about prayer?

Reflect

- Do you think Jesus' blessing prayer for the children really made a difference in their lives? What blessings might they have received?

- How do children get Jesus' blessing today?

- What are the most important things we should ask for our family members and friends?

Apply

- Did anyone pray for you when you were a child? How do you know?

- Who among your family or friends does God want you to pray for with "shameless audacity"?

Praying for My Spiritual Family

"My *prayer* is not for them [Jesus' followers] alone. *I pray* also for those who will believe in me through their message, that all of them may be one, Father, just as you are in me and I am in you. May they also be in us so that the world may believe that you have sent me." –Jn. 17:20-21

For this reason, since the day we heard about you, we have *not stopped praying* for you. We *continually ask* God to fill you with the knowledge of his will through all the wisdom and understanding that the Spirit gives, so that you may live a life worthy of the Lord and please him in every way: bearing fruit in every good work, growing in the knowledge of God, being strengthened with all power according to his glorious might so that you may have great endurance and patience, giving joyful thanks to the Father.
–Col. 1:9-12

Epaphras, who is one of you and a servant of Christ Jesus, sends greetings. He is *always wrestling in prayer* for you, that you may stand firm in all the will of God, mature and fully assured. –Col. 4:12

Pray for each other. . . .The prayer of a righteous person is powerful and effective. –James 5:16

Discover
- Who is Jesus praying for in John 17:20? What did he ask the Father to do for them?

- What will bring a church to the point where it lives a life worthy of the Lord and pleases him in every way?

- What will characterize a church that lives a life worthy of the Lord and pleases him? Try to put this in four words.

Reflect
- What would you expect to see in a church if its members have a oneness like that of the Father and the Son?

- What do the prayers of Jesus, Paul and Epaphras teach us about praying for the family of God?

- What was the *power* that James credited to prayer? Where did it come from? What did it accomplish? How was it activated?

Apply
- Do you think your prayers can be as powerful and effective as those of Paul and Epaphras? Why or why not?

- How do your prayers for your church compare, in intensity and content, to those of Paul and Epaphras?

Praying for Effective Ministry

"Very truly I tell you, whoever believes in me will do the works I have been doing, and they will do even greater things than these, because I am going to the Father. And I will do *whatever you ask* in my name, so that the Father may be glorified in the Son. You *may ask* me for anything in my name, and I will do it." –Jn. 14:12-14

"If you remain in me and my words remain in you, ask whatever you wish, and it will be done for you. This is to my Father's glory, that you bear much fruit, showing yourselves to be my disciples. . . .You did not choose me, but I chose you and appointed you so that you might go and bear fruit—fruit that will last—and so that whatever you ask in my name the Father will give you." –Jn. 15:7-8, 16

Discover
- What, according to Jesus, is the connection between prayer and effective ministry?

- What did Christ's choosing and appointing disciples have to do with prayer and effective ministry?

- How will our fruit-bearing ministries affect the Father?

Reflect
- Why will Christ-followers bear fruit that will last?

- What does it mean to pray "in Jesus name"? Why is that important?

Apply
- What will happen to our ministry efforts if we neglect prayer? Why?

- How much fruit are you bearing for Christ? Is there a way that you could produce more fruit?

Praying for Spiritual Leaders

"I pray for them [my disciples]. I am not praying for the world, but for those you have given me, for they are yours.... My prayer is not that you take them out of the world but that you protect them from the evil one.... Sanctify them by the truth; your word is truth." –Jn. 17:9, 15, 17

Paul . . . to Philemon our dear friend and fellow worker... I always *thank my God* as I *remember you* in my prayers, because I hear about your love for all his holy people and your faith in the Lord Jesus. I *pray* that your partnership with us in the faith may be effective in deepening your understanding of every good thing we share for the sake of Christ. –Philem. 1, 4-6

As for other matters, brothers and sisters, *pray for us* [Paul, Silas and Timothy] that the message of the Lord may spread rapidly and be honored, just as it was with you. And pray that we may be delivered from wicked and evil people, for not everyone has faith. –2 Thess. 3:1-2

Discover
- What do the prayers of Jesus and Paul teach us about praying for spiritual leaders?

- What burden gave rise to Paul's prayer request for himself and his companions? What alarm did he sound?

Reflect
- What do you think the Father does when he hears a prayer for protection from the evil one and for sanctification?

- What kinds of perils do today's spiritual leaders face? What kinds of opportunities?

Apply
- How are your prayers for leaders like or unlike those of Jesus and Paul?

- What do these verses teach us about praying for pastors, missionaries and evangelists?

Bottom Line Questions
1. What is the single most important idea you are taking away from this *pray-for-family-and-friends-in-Christ* study?

2. What, practically, might a well-developed *pray-for-family-and-friends-in-Christ* prayer habit look like in a believer's life today?

Summing Up

Are you impressed by the prayers of Paul, Epaphras, and Jesus? I surely am. They are amazing intercessory prayers, flowing from hearts full of love and a deep concern for the spiritual well-being of believer-friends. But something far more impressive than the prayers are the God-answers that come out of those prayers. God, who heard Paul's prayers for the Colossians, *did fill* them with the knowledge of his will through the wisdom and understanding of the Holy Spirit. God, who heard Epaphras's prayers, *did help* the believers stand firm in his will. The Father, who heard the prayers of his Son, *did give* the disciples a unity like that between him and his Son. The most amazing thing about our prayers are the God-answers.

As you pray for family and friends in Christ, be impressed by God's willingness and ability to do what you ask. He is willing and able to help your friends in Christ by your prayers. He is willing and able to protect them from the evil one, and to sanctify them in the truth. You know believers who need what only God can give. And God, for reasons only he understands perfectly, has decided to give them in response to your asking. God has made you his partner in grace. That is amazing!

Four Steps to Develop the Habit of *Praying for Family and Friends In Christ*

1. Set the Stage for *Praying for Family and Friends In Christ.*

- Place yourself under the authority of God's Word in James 5:16. Tell God you will do what he commands. Affirm the powerful effect your prayers will have. Memorize and think of this verse often when you pray for family and friends in Christ.

    "Pray for each other. . . .The prayer of a righteous person is powerful and effective." –James 5:16

- Make a real or a good mental lists of . . .
    . . . family members for whom you will pray daily:

    . . . friends of faith for whom you will pray regularly (small group members, colleagues in ministry, persons with special needs, etc.):

    . . . the spiritual family for whom you choose to pray often (church, denomination, ministry organization, etc.)

- Use Paul's powerful and comprehensive prayer for the Colossians (1:9-11) as a model for your prayers for family and friends in Christ. If you pray this daily for a couple of weeks you will have it memorized. To widen the scope of "one another" prayers go on to use other passages like Ephesians 1:16-19, 3:15-19; Philippians 1:9-11; and Numbers 6:24-26.

2. Detect Habits that May Hinder *Praying for Family and Friends in Christ.*

Which of the following habits may hinder your *praying for family and friends in Christ?*

___ When praying for fellow believers I am more inclined to pray fix-it prayers than grow-in-grace prayers (Col. 4:12).

___ I often pray quick and easy prayers without much passion or follow-through (Lk.11:5-8).

___ My prayers do not regularly reflect the conviction that believers can "do the works that Jesus did," as he does what we ask in his name (Jn. 14:12-14).

___ When everything seems to be going well for with my family and friends I seldom think to pray for them (Job. 1:4-5).

___ I don't naturally thank God for people the way spiritual giants from Scripture did (1 Thess. 1:1-3).

3. Launch the *Pray-for-Family-and-Friends-In-Christ* Habit with a Prayer.

- ♦ *Thank* God for his willingness to bless others in response to your prayers.
- ♦ *Repent* of any hindering habits (above) that may keep you from *praying for family and friends in Christ.*
- ♦ *Ask* God to make you the intercessor for others that he wants you to be.
- ♦ *Commit* yourself to a place and time to intercede for family and friends in Christ.
- ♦ *Pray for* family members and friends in Christ, using thoughts and words from the verses we have just studied.

4. Lock In *Praying for Family and Friends In Christ* as a Lifetime Habit.

⇒ *Set aside* a time every day in which you can intercede for family and friends in Christ.

⇒ Regularly repeat the *thank-repent-tell-ask-commit-pray for* steps from the personal *praying-for-family-&-friends-in-Christ* prayer time above.

⇒ Watch for and rejoice in God's answers to your prayers (2 Cor. 1:10-11).

⇒ Expand your use of prayer themes that you can garner from great prayers of the Bible.

Group Prayer and Covenant Time

The Entire Group Prepares for and Prays Personal Prayers of Confession and Petition

- Each person selects one **hindering habit**—one you marked in step 2 above—to bring to the whole group prayer time.
- Group members **take one minute** to consider the negative effects of that hindrance and reflect on (or write down) what positive change to ask God for:

_____

_____

- Each person contributes a **two-sentence prayer**: one sentence to confess the hindering habit, and a second sentence to claim God's grace to develop a "right" habit. (Leaders go first.)

The Whole Group Covenants Together Aloud and in Unison

"In utter dependence upon Jesus Christ as my ever-living Savior, Teacher, Lord and prayer partner, I will regularly practice the prayer habit of praying for family and friends in Christ and will prayerfully support the others in our Seven Habits group in their pursuit of effective prayer habits."

Small Group Share and Prayer Time
(The session ends with this exercise.)

- Each person writes down:
  A prayer request for the help you may want to develop the habit of ***praying for family and friends in Christ***:

  _____
  _____

  Another prayer request for yourself or for one other person:

  _____
  _____

- Each person shares, in two or three sentences, the above two prayer requests with their small group of 2-4 persons.

- Each person prays for one other person in the group covering the two requests just shared.

AFTER SESSION SEVEN

Pray for Each Other
Pray for the members of your group, especially your small group, every day with the understanding that things will happen in their prayer lives if you pray for them that won't happen if you don't pray.

Pray about Your Prayer Life
Review key Scripture passages from session seven. Pray about your commitment to pray for others. Watch carefully for God's leadings. Are there believers among your family and friends who need more prayer support? Are there other believers who need more prayer covering? What spiritual leaders would profit from your intense prayers?

Develop the "Pray for Family and Friends In Christ" Prayer Habit

◊ *Ask* God to make you a faithful intercessor, giving you a loving concern for those you pray for, discernment of their needs, an awareness of what he wants to do in their lives, and the faith to ask boldly and persistently, releasing his power and grace into their lives.

◊ *Pray one of Paul's prayers* for your family of God every day for a week (Eph. 1:16-19, 3:16-20; Phil. 1:9-11; Col. 1:9-11; 2 Thess. 1:11-12). Choose a different prayer for each week; repeat the cycle every five weeks. There will be a great advantage to memorizing these prayers of Paul and the character quality passages referenced above.

◊ *Pray for the leaders* of your local congregation: the pastoral staff, ministry leaders, worship leaders, teachers, counselors, small group leaders, missionaries, administrators, and so on. Pray with a consciousness of their ministry roles, opportunities, challenges, relationships, temptations.

◊ *Pray an expanded version of the Lord's Prayer,* asking that those you pray for may be able to glorify God's name, advance his kingdom, do his will, be provided for, find forgiveness and be delivered from the evil one.

SESSION 8

Habit Seven: **Pray for Neighbors and Nations**

"God has placed the destiny of the world in the hands of believers. Yes, this is God's world, but he has given us a responsibility for what happens in it. He has authorized us to rule the world along with his Son. The most critical element of our ongoing 'rule' is sustained, fervent, intercessory prayer. God can bless the world through our intercessory prayers."[1] God wants his will to be done on earth as it is done in heaven (Matt. 6:10), and prayer is an indispensable part of making that happen. Eugene Peterson writes, "Far more of our nation's life is shaped by prayer than is formed by legislation. That we have not collapsed into anarchy is due more to prayer than to the police. . . . That society continues to be livable and that hope continues to be resurgent are attributable more to prayer far more than to business prosperity or a flourishing of the arts. The single most important action contributing to whatever health and strength there is in our land is prayer."[2]

Praying for neighbors and nations means this: finding out what God wants to happen, and praying for that. God wants all people to love and serve him, to become part of his kingdom. That's God's vision. And prayer is the channel through which it happens. Prayer can reach your family members, friends, neighbors and coworkers. Prayer can reach your town, city, state and nation. Prayer can reach into every one of the 237 nations of the world. Every one of us can be part of that "reach" through our prayers.

Jesus, now on the throne of the universe, is still as compassionately concerned for the unsaved as he was in his days on earth. He is asking the Father to make the nations of the earth his inheritance (Ps. 2:8). But he does not pray alone. We pray with him for those who will reap the ripening harvest fields of the earth (Matt. 9:38). We pray with him who "wants all people to be saved and to come to a knowledge of the truth," making petitions, prayers, intercession and thanksgiving for all people, knowing that "this is good, and pleases God our Savior" (1 Tim. 2:1-4).

As you meditate on the following verses, let your heart beat alongside the heart of God. Feel God's grief at not finding an intercessor to stand in the gap for erring Israel. Sense the Father's compassion for hurting people as Jesus expresses heartfelt concern for harassed and helpless "sheep." Tap into God's concern for the unsaved as Paul prays his heart's desire for Israel. Let Malachi's strong desire that the name of God "be great among the nations" inspire your prayers for neighbors and nations today. Be the intercessor God has meant you to be. Make a difference for God's here-and-now kingdom.

---

[1] Vander Griend, *Praying God's Heart*, p. 111.
[2] *Where Your Treasure Is*, p. 6.

Bible Study for "Pray for Neighbors and Nations"

Note that all italics below were inserted by the author of this study.

Praying for the Unsaved

When [Jesus] saw the crowds, he had compassion on them, because they were harassed and helpless, like sheep without a shepherd. Then he said to his disciples, "The harvest is plentiful but the workers are few. *Ask the Lord* of the harvest, therefore, to send out workers into his harvest field."–Matt. 9:36-38

I [Paul] have great sorrow and unceasing anguish in my heart. For I could wish that I myself were cursed and cut off from Christ for the sake of my people, those of my own race.... Brothers and sisters, my heart's desire and prayer to God for the Israelites is that *they may be saved.* –Rom. 9:2-3; 10:1

I urge, then, first of all, that petitions, prayers, intercession and thanksgiving be made for *all people*.... This is good, and pleases God our Savior, who wants all people *to be saved* and to come to a knowledge of the truth. –1 Tim. 2:1, 3-4

Discover
- What did Jesus and Paul feel that made them think of prayer as a solution?

- What did Paul think would happen if prayer "for all people" became a high priority?

- What do these passages teach us about prayer for the unsaved?

Reflect
- What are some ways that God might answer today if we faithfully pray for harvest workers?

- Do you think the harvest is still plentiful today? What needs to happen when a field is ripe for harvest?

Apply
- Do you know persons that are "harassed and helpless, like sheep without a shepherd"? What are your feelings about their situation?

- What could you do to make a difference in their lives?

Praying for an Erring Nation

"If my people, who are called by my name, will humble themselves *and pray* and seek my face and turn from their wicked ways, then I will hear from heaven, and I will forgive their sin and will heal their land. Now my eyes will be open and my ears attentive to the prayers offered in this place." –2 Chron. 7:14-15

They forgot the God who saved them, who had done great things in Egypt, miracles in the land of Ham. . . . So he said he would destroy them -- had not Moses, his chosen one, *stood in the breach* before him to keep his wrath from destroying them. –Ps. 106:21, 23

"I looked for someone among them who would *build up the wall* and *stand before me in the gap* on behalf of the land so I would not have to destroy [Israel], but I found no one. So I will pour out my wrath on them and consume them with my fiery anger, bringing down on their own heads all they have done," declares the Sovereign LORD. –Ezek. 22:30-31

Discover

- When things are going wrong in a nation, what is the first step people need to take? The second? The third? The fourth? What is God's promise to those who take these steps? (2 Chron. 7:14-15)

- How did erring Israel get spared in Moses' day? How did God think to resolve the problem of Israel's wickedness in Ezekiel's day? Why didn't it work?

Reflect

- What does it mean for someone to "stand in the gap" or "stand in the breach" before God on behalf of a nation?

- Do you think God's wrathful response would have been averted in Ezekiel's day if he had found an intercessor to stand in the gap? Would your answer apply today?

Apply

- Do the promises of God to those who "humble themselves and pray and seek his face" still apply today? Why or why not?

- Do you think God is looking for intercessors to pray for your country right now? Are you willing to step in to that gap?

Praying for Rulers and Nations

I urge, then, first of all, that *petitions, prayers, intercession and thanksgiving* be made for all people - for kings and all those in authority, that we may live peaceful and quiet lives in all godliness and holiness. –1 Tim. 2:1-2

I will proclaim the LORD's decree: He said to me, "You are my son; today I have become your father. *Ask* me, and I will make the nations your inheritance, the ends of the earth your possession." –Ps. 2:7-8

"Also, seek the peace and prosperity of the city to which I have carried you into exile. *Pray* to the LORD for it, because if it prospers, you too will prosper." –Jer. 29:7

Discover
- What is God's vision for the nations of the world?

- How does God's Son figure into the Lord's vision for the world?

- What quality of life can be expected in a nation where believers faithfully pray for "kings and all in authority"?

Reflect
- Do you think that the prayers of God's people can bring peace and prosperity in a city that, like Babylon, is otherwise godless?

- What changes do you think we would see in our country if we consistently prayed as urged by Paul in 1 Tim. 2:1-2?

Apply
- What is our role in making the nations of the world the inheritance of Christ? (Ps. 2:7-8)

- How have you been led to pray for your city, state or nation?

God's Heart for the Nations

May God be gracious to us and bless us and make his face shine on us - so that your ways may be known on earth, your salvation among all nations. May the peoples praise you, God; may all the peoples praise you. May the nations be glad and sing for joy, for you rule the peoples with equity and guide the nations of the earth. May *the peoples praise you*, God; may all the peoples praise you.... May God bless us still, so that all the ends of the earth will fear him.
–Ps. 67:1-5, 7

"My *name* will be *great among the nations*, from where the sun rises to where it sets. In every place incense and pure offerings will be brought to me, because my name will be great among the nations," says the LORD Almighty." – Mal. 1:11

Then Jesus came to them and said, "All authority in heaven and on earth has been given to me. Therefore go and *make disciples of all nations*, baptizing them in the name of the Father and of the Son and of the Holy Spirit, and teaching them to obey everything I have commanded you. And surely I am with you always, to the very end of the age."
–Matt. 28:19-20

Discover
- Why, according to Psalm 67, should we ask God to "be gracious to us and bless us"?

- What is God's great desire for the nations of the world?

- How does God expect the nations to respond to him once his ways are known on earth?

- What does Christ expect us to do for the nations? What hope do we have of succeeding?

Reflect
- When we pray, what difference does it make for us to know that Jesus Christ has "all authority in heaven and on earth"?

- What is the difference between making converts and making disciples? What will characterize a true disciple?

Apply
- What, if anything, has God taught you about praying his heart for the nations of the world?

Bottom Line Questions
1. What is the single most important idea you are taking away from this *pray-for-neighbors-and-nations* study?

2. What, practically, might a well-developed *pray-for-neighbors-and-nations* prayer habit look like in a believer's life today?

Summing Up
The prayers of believers shape history. History was shaped when Jewish exiles prayed for the cities into which they were carried into exile. History was shaped when the disciples prayed for the Lord of the harvest to send out workers into the harvest field. History was shaped when Paul prayed for the salvation of fellow Israelites.

History will be shaped when God—who looks for believers to stand in the gap—finds you. People will be saved and come to a knowledge of the truth when you make requests, prayers, intercession, and thanksgiving for all people. Great things—even greater than those things that Christ did—will be accomplished when Jesus does what you ask in his name.
In a very real sense the future of the world is in the hands of praying Christians. So is the future of your neighborhood, the future of your church, and the future of your community. I hope and pray that your prayers will contribute to a glorious future for the kingdom of God right where you live, and work and pray.

Four Steps to Develop the Habit of *Praying for Neighbors and Nations*

1. Set the Stage for *Praying for Neighbors and Nations.*
- Can you agree with Paul's idea in 1 Timothy 2:1-4, that prayer for neighbors and nations is high priority and very urgent? The results of faithful prayer for the rulers of nations and for the unsaved are spectacular. Hang these words on the walls of your heart and memorize them as you commit to pray for neighbors and nations.

    "First of all, then, I urge that entreaties and prayers, petitions and thanksgivings, be made on behalf of all men, for kings and all who are in authority, so that we may lead a tranquil and quiet life in all godliness and dignity. This is good and acceptable in the sight of God our Savior, who desires all men to be saved and to come to the knowledge of the truth." –1 Tim. 2:1-4

- Make a list of:
    - Family members, friends, neighbors or fellow workers who are not Christ-followers: _____, _____, _____, _____, _____, _____, _____.

    - Key leaders of your:
      City/Town/Village: _____
      State: _____
      Nation: _____

    - Nation(s) for which God might want you to pray (these might be nations about which you have some knowledge): _____, _____, _____, _____.

2. Detect Habits That May Hinder *Praying for Neighbors and Nations.*

Which of the following habits may hinder your *praying for neighbors and nations?*

___ I have not been concerned enough about the salvation of unsaved people I know to pray for them (Rom.10:1).

___ I haven't been asking the Lord of the harvest to send out workers into his harvest field, as Jesus commanded in Matthew 9:37.

___ I have not been serious about making "requests, prayers, intercessions and thanksgiving . . . for kings and all those in authority" (1 Tim. 1:1-2).

___ I have not given much thought to the need for me to "stand in the gap" for my nation because of rampant evil (Ezek. 22:30-31).

___ I find it hard to believe that my little prayers can make a difference for a whole city or nation (Jer. 29:7).

3. Launch the *Praying for Neighbors and Nations* Habit with a Prayer.

- *Thank* God for his willingness to use you and your prayers to shape the lives of neighbors and nations (Ps. 106:23).
- *Repent* of any hindering habits that may keep you from *praying neighbors and nations.* Review on occasion the Scripture references that remind you of God's prayer expectations.
- *Ask* God to give you a passionate concern for the salvation of neighbors and a widening concern to "make the nations [Christ's] inheritance" (Ps. 2:8).
- *Commit* yourself to pray for neighbors and nations as the Spirit prompts you (Eph.6:18).

4. Lock in *Praying for Neighbors and Nations* as a Lifetime Habit.

⇒ Keep the list of unsaved friends, political leaders, and nations that you created in step 1 above in a place that will remind you to pray over them regularly.

⇒ Regularly repeat the *thank-repent-tell-ask-commit* steps from the personal *praying-for-neighbors-and-nations* prayer time above.

⇒ Review occasionally the Scripture passages referenced in the "possible hindrances" section to lock in the importance of *praying for neighbors and nations.*

Group Prayer and Covenant Time

The Entire Group Prepares for and Prays Personal Prayers of Confession and Petition

- Each person selects one **hindering habit**—one you marked in step 2 above—to bring to the whole group prayer time.
- Group members **take one minute** to consider the negative effects of that hindrance and reflect on (or write down) what positive change to ask God for:

_____

_____

- In a whole group prayer time each person contributes a **two-sentence prayer**: one sentence to confess the hindering habit, and a second sentence to claim God's grace to develop a "right" habit. (Leaders go first.)

The Whole Group Covenants Together Aloud and In Unison

"In utter dependence upon Jesus Christ as my ever-living Savior, Teacher, Lord and prayer partner, I will regularly practice the prayer habit of praying for neighbors and nations and will prayerfully support the others in our Seven Habits group in their pursuit of effective prayer habits."

Small Group Share and Prayer Time
(The session ends with this exercise.)

- Each person writes down:
  A prayer request for the help you may want to develop the habit of *praying for neighbors and nations*:

  _____
  _____

  Another prayer request for yourself or for one other person:

  _____
  _____

- Each person shares, in two or three sentences, the above two prayer requests with their small group of 2-4 persons.

- Each person prays for one other person in the group covering the two requests just shared.

AFTER SESSION EIGHT

Pray for Others
Pray for the members of your small group each day, with the understanding that things will happen in their prayer lives if you pray that wouldn't have happened if you hadn't prayed.

Pray about Your Prayer Life
Review key Scripture passages from session eight. Pray about your own *pray-for-neighbors-and-nations* prayer habit. Practice this habit daily. Watch carefully for God's leadings. Are there neighbors or nations now being covered that weren't covered before?

Develop the "Pray for Neighbors and Nations" Prayer Habit

◊ Ask God to make you *a faithful intercessor.* Pray that he may give you a loving concern for unsaved friends and neighbors and a keen awareness of what he wants to do in their lives. Pray for the faith to be a bold and persistent "friend in the middle" (Luke 11:5-8).

◊ Keep a written *"Most Wanted Persons" list* of unsaved persons whom God lays on your heart. Regularly pray the ABC prayer prompts, asking that they **admit** their need to be forgiven of sin, **believe** in Jesus Christ and be saved, and **commit** to love and serve the Lord.

◊ Pray for *unsaved persons*, using one or more of the following Scripture passages:
    That God will draw them to himself (John 6:44)
    That they hear the message (Rom. 10:17)
    That God will send someone to lead them to Christ (Matt. 9:37-38)
    That they believe the word of Christ (John 5:24)

◊ Pray on behalf of *our nation*:
    Pray for our president, senators and representatives.
    Pray for the peoples of our land.
    Pray for enemies.

SESSION 9

Be a Prayer-Devoted Church

William Carey writes, "Prayer—secret, fervent, believing, prayer—lies at the root of all personal godliness." If that be true, then we will not only want to develop the habits of effective prayer for ourselves, but want to foster devotion to prayer in the lives of our family members, friends, small groups, and churches.

Jesus and the early church leaders found effective ways to encourage prayer. First, they *modeled* prayer in a way that made it appealing. The disciples were so impressed by Jesus' prayer life that they said, "Lord, teach us to pray." The writer of Hebrews testified that "during the days of his life on earth, Jesus offered up prayers and petitions with loud cries and tears." Shortly before his arrest Jesus prayed aloud to his Father as the disciples listened (Jn. 17). No wonder, then, that at the very beginning of their ministry Jesus' disciples deliberately planned to give their attention to prayer as well as to the ministry of the word.

Second, spiritual leaders promoted prayer by *teaching*. Jesus gave his disciples a pattern for prayer: the Lord's Prayer. He taught them the value of corporate prayer by promising that "if two of you on earth agree about anything you ask for, it will be done for you by my Father in heaven." Paul taught believers to "pray in the Spirit on all occasions with all kinds of prayers and requests" and to "always keep on praying for all God's people." James endorsed prayer as the proper response in times of trouble, happiness, sickness, or sin, and stressed that "the prayer of a righteous person is powerful and effective."

Third, early church leaders fostered prayer by *urging* their followers to pray. Jesus, concerned for harassed and helpless "sheep," urged his followers to "ask the Lord of harvest…to send out workers into his harvest field." Later he urged his sleeping disciples to "watch and pray so that you will not fall into temptation." Paul urged his spiritual son Timothy to make sure that requests, prayers, intercession and thanksgiving were made for everyone.

Finally, early church leaders fostered prayer by bringing people together in *united prayer*. Following the threats of the chief priests and elders, the disciples called a prayer meeting in which they all "raised their voices together in prayer to God." The early church was characterized by united prayer. Thirteen of the prayers recorded in the book of Acts were times of corporate prayer. Churches nurtured by praying leaders became devoted to prayer. So it was and so it ever shall be!

In this series of verses you will be hearing not simply what the Spirit is saying about prayer, but what the Spirit is saying about prayer *to the church*. Don't settle simply for personal devotion to prayer. Press on to become a prayer-devoted church.

Bible Study for "Be a Prayer-Devoted Church"

Note that all italics below were inserted by the author of this study.

This Is How We Should Pray

"This, then, is *how you should pray*: 'Our Father in heaven, hallowed be your name, your kingdom come, your will be done, on earth as it is in heaven. Give us today our daily bread. And forgive us our debts, as we also have forgiven our debtors. And lead us not into temptation, but deliver us from the evil one.'" –Matt. 6:9-13

And pray in the Spirit on all occasions with all kinds of prayers and requests. With this in mind, be alert and always keep on praying for all the Lord's people. Pray also for me, that whenever I speak, words may be given me so that I will fearlessly make known the mystery of the gospel. . . .Pray that I may declare it fearlessly, as I should. –Eph. 6:18-20

Is anyone among you in trouble? Let them pray. Is anyone happy? Let them sing songs of praise. Is anyone among you sick? Let them call the elders of the church to pray over them and anoint them with oil in the name of the Lord. And the prayer offered in faith will make the sick person well; the Lord will raise them up. If they have sinned, they will be forgiven. Therefore confess your sins to each other and pray for each other so that you may be healed. The prayer of a righteous person is powerful and effective. –James 5:13-16

I *urge*, then, first of all, that petitions, prayers, intercession and thanksgiving be made for all people. –1 Tim. 2:1

Discover
- Each of these passages urges us to pray. How are they similar? How are they different?

- If believers pray in the way these verses suggest, who gets prayed for?

- Whose concerns are primary in the Lord's Prayer? What does this teach us about prayer?

Reflect
- There are nine plural pronouns in the Lord's Prayer. What does this tell us about Jesus' concept of prayer?

- James mentions several different life situations (5:13-16). How do the life situations affect the kind of prayers prayed? What is his primary lesson?

Apply
- What would the prayer life of a congregation look like if all of these instructions on prayer were taken seriously?

Praying-Devoted Leaders

One day *Jesus was praying* in a certain place. When he finished, one of his disciples said to him, "Lord, teach us to pray, just as John taught his disciples." –Luke 11:1

During the days of Jesus' life on earth, he *offered up prayers and petitions* with fervent cries and tears to the one who could save him from death, and he was heard because of his reverent submission. –Heb. 5:7

"Brothers and sisters, choose seven men from among you who are known to be full of the Spirit and wisdom. We will turn this responsibility over to them and will *give our attention to prayer* and the ministry of the word." –Acts 6:3-4

I thank my God every time I remember you. In *all my prayers* for all of you, I *always pray* with joy because of your partnership in the gospel from the first day until now. –Phil. 1:3-5

I have not *stopped giving thanks* for you, remembering you in *my prayers*. I *keep asking* that the God of our Lord Jesus Christ, the glorious Father, may give you the Spirit of wisdom and revelation, so that you may know him better. –Eph. 1:16-17

Discover
- What level of priority did prayer have in the lives of Jesus, his twelve disciples, and the apostle Paul?

- What is there in these verses to suggest that their devotion to prayer was a lifetime commitment (a habit), not just a passing phase?

- How did Jesus' disciples avoid getting too busy to pray?

Reflect
- What impact did Jesus' prayer life have on the disciples?

- What impact do you think that the apostles' commitment to prayer had on early believers? (Acts 6:3-4)

Apply
- How can that kind of impact exerted by these early church leaders be replicated in the church today?

- Who has modeled prayer for you? For whom is your prayer life a model?

The Prayer-Devoted Church

"Again, truly I tell you that if two of you on earth agree about *anything* they ask for [*themselves*], it will be done for them by my Father in heaven. For where two or three gather in my name, there am I with them." –Matt. 18:19-20

These all with one mind were continually *devoting themselves to prayer*, along with the women, and Mary the mother of Jesus, and with His brothers.
–Acts 1:14 (NASB)

Then they [the Sanhedrin] . . . commanded them not to speak or teach at all in the name of Jesus. . . . On their release, Peter and John went back to their own people and reported all that the chief priests and the elders had said to them. When they heard this, they raised their voices *together in prayer* to God. . . "Now, Lord, consider their threats and enable your servants to speak your word with great boldness. Stretch out your hand to heal and perform signs and wonders through the name of your holy servant Jesus." After *they prayed*, the place where they were meeting was shaken. And they were all filled with the Holy Spirit and spoke the word of God boldly.
–Acts 4:18, 23-24, 29-31

Devote yourselves to prayer, being watchful and thankful.
–Col. 4:2

Discover
- What is there to suggest that the Jerusalem church was truly devoted to prayer?

- What two great blessings are promised to believers who agree in prayer?

- What can we learn about united prayer from the Jerusalem church?

Reflect
- What might make you think that Jesus really wanted his church to be devoted to communal prayer?

- How can believers find agreement in prayer? (Matt. 18:19-20)

- Why do you think God shook the building after the Jerusalem church prayed?

Apply
- What can pastors and church leaders do to encourage more united prayer? What results might come from that?

- Would you like to be part of a church that had prayer meetings like that of the Jerusalem church? Why or why not?

Bottom Line Questions
1. What is the single most important idea you are taking away from this *be-a-prayer-devoted-church* study?

2. What, practically, might a church do to become more *devoted to* prayer?

Summing Up

The first Christians were truly devoted to prayer. They didn't just pray personal prayers at home; they came together for prayer. They didn't just pray for health and welfare; they labored in prayer for the advance of the kingdom. Their prayers were not quick and easy. They occupied themselves diligently with prayer. They were watchful and constant, persistent in prayer. Their prayers laid the foundation for the explosive growth of the New Testament church. Their prayers paved the way for the church we are part of today.

That is the kind of prayer that God expects of his church. The great Christian leader Chrysostom once said, "God can refuse nothing to a praying congregation." He meant not just a congregation that prays, but a congregation that is devoted to prayer. Is that the kind of congregation you are? That's a question worth asking.

Four Steps to Becoming a Prayer-Devoted Church

1. Set the Stage for Your Church to Become Fully *Devoted to Prayer.*

- Paul is instructing a church, not an individual, in Colossians 4:2 when he challenges, *"Devote yourselves to prayer, being watchful and thankful."* Ask yourself, "How can I help my church to become fully devoted to prayer?" Carry Colossians 4:2 in your heart as you consider your role as a church member.

- Assess the current state of prayer in your congregation:
  Is there a leadership team? (_____)
  Is prayer integrated into the ministries of the church? (_____)
  Are we communicating prayer needs, answers, and opportunities for prayer? (_____)

See **"About the Course"** in the back of this book, #4, "Becoming a Prayer-Devoted Church" for ideas on how to help your church become (or remain) fully devoted to prayer.

2. Help Your Church Detect Habits that May Hinder Its *Devotion to Prayer.*
Which of the following habits may hinder your church's *devotion to prayer?*
___We have made prayer more about problem-solving than kingdom-building.
___We have succumbed to a culturally induced busyness that has left little time for prayer.
___We have placed too much confidence in our own human efforts.
___We haven't understood the importance of corporate prayer.
___Many of our members are afraid to pray aloud in public.

3. Launch Your Church on the Road to Becoming Fully *Devoted to Prayer.*
- *Thank* God for the prayer-devotion model of the New Testament church. Thank him also for the amount of prayer you do see in your church.
- *Confess* any hindrances to church prayer-devotion (from step 2 above) and decide how to reverse course.
- *Ask* God to help your church become as devoted to prayer as he wants you to be.
- *Commit* to doing what you can to move your church forward in devotion to prayer.

4. Continue to Help Your Church Become Fully *Devoted to Prayer.*
⇒ Continue to develop your own prayer habits. See **About the Course #1**, "Honing Your Prayer Habits."
⇒ Form or join an affinity prayer group. See **About the Course #2**, "Finding an Affinity Prayer Group."
⇒ Pursue the "Becoming a Prayer-Devoted Church" goals found in **About the Course #3**.
⇒ Be prepared to step into prayer ministries or prayer leadership roles in your church.
⇒ Consider forming and leading another *Seven Habits of Effective Prayer* group. See **Leader Helps**, "Forming a *Seven Habits* Class" and "Leading a *Seven Habits* Class."
⇒ **Continue** to ask God to help your church become fully devoted to prayer.

Group Prayer

Prayer prompted by the leader:

◊ **Leader:** Remembering the prayer habit of *claiming God's riches*, let's together claim spiritual riches for ourselves and for our friends in Christ.

- Two or more group members prayerfully claim spiritual riches.

◊ **Leader:** Remembering the prayer habit of *giving God glory*, let's together praise and thank our faithful God and Father.

- Two or more group members lead out in prayers of praise and thanksgiving.

◊ **Leader:** Remembering the prayer habit of *seeking God's face*, let's pray that we individually and as a church deeply desire an intimate, face-to-face relationship with God.

- Two or more members pray for "soul thirst," longing, and greater desire for the Lord.

◊ **Leader:** Remembering the prayer habit of *winning over sin*, let's pray for pardon for sins we have committed and for power over temptation.

- Two or more members pray for *victory* over anything that the world, the flesh, and the devil might do to trap us in sinful life patterns.

◊ **Leader:** Remembering the prayer habit of *hearing God's voice*, let's pray for ears to hear what God is saying through his Word and Spirit.

- Two or three members pray that God enable us to hear every word that comes from the mouth of God.

◊ **Leader:** Remembering the prayer habit of *praying for family & friends in Christ*, let's be a 'friend in the middle,' asking God to pour down his blessing on fellow believers.

- Two or more members pray for our families, our friends of faith, our churches, and our spiritual leaders.

◊ **Leader:** Remembering the prayer habit of *praying for neighbors and nations*, let's intercede on behalf of our world.

- Two or more members pray for unsaved persons, for the advance of the kingdom of God, for kings and those in authority, and for the spread of the gospel to the whole world.

◊ **Leader:** Finally, let's pray that our churches will become truly *devoted to prayer*.

- Two or more members pray that fellow Christians will more and more be able to "pray in the Spirit on all occasions with all kinds of prayers and requests . . . and always keep on praying for all God's people."

◊ **Leader:** We close our time together by praying the Lord's Prayer aloud and in unison:

Our Father in heaven, hallowed be your name, your kingdom come, your will be done, on earth as it is in heaven. Give us today our daily bread. And forgive us our debts, as we also have forgiven our debtors. And lead us not into temptation, but deliver us from the evil one. Yours is the kingdom, the power, and the glory. Amen

---

Group Wrap-Up Time

Do a quick overview of the following appendices:

⇒ "Memory Verses for the Seven Habits course." Memorizing these verses will help you remember and use the key ideas in the *Seven Habits* course in the future.

⇒ "Seven Habits Prayer Guide." These simple prayers will keep you on target as you move forward in the seven habits of prayer.

⇒ "Bonus Session." **About the Course #5**. The class may choose to use this format for a follow-up session in which returning class members share the progress they have made, ask questions that have come up, and encourage and pray with each other as they move forward on their way to more robust prayer lives.

THE WEEKS AHEAD

Make the *Seven Habits of Effective Prayer* a Lifestyle.

Watch carefully for progress in each of the seven prayer habits. Keep asking questions like:

- 1st – Am I experiencing more and more of God's blessings as I *claim God's riches* every day?
- 2nd – What's happening in my relationship with God as I spend significant time *giving him glory* each day?
- 3rd – Am I really getting *face-to-face time* with God? Is this helping me be more conscious of God throughout each day?
- 4th – Am I *overcoming sin* and winning new victories over the world, the flesh and the devil every day?
- 5th – Have I been able to *hear God* better and enjoy conversation with him lately?
- 6th – Do I really have a sense of co-laboring with God in behalf of *friends in Christ* and making a difference in their lives?
- 7th – Am I getting more and more of God's heart for my *neighbors and the nations of the world*?

Review the Nine Sessions in the Next 30 Days.

- Rereading the introduction to each of the sessions will give you a quick overview of the Bible's perspective on each prayer habit.
- Thoughtfully reviewing the selected Bible passages will deepen your conviction regarding the prayer habits.
- Reviewing and retrying each of the practice steps could help you improve a prayer habit.
- The "Weeks Ahead" section at the end of each session suggest new ways to make each prayer habit a reality.

Appendices

- ~ About the Course
- ~ Leader Helps
- ~ Personal Guides

Appendix

About the Course

Goals and Values of the Course

Goals of the *Seven Habits* course
1. Christ-followers will be able to develop effective prayer lives by locking in seven key, everyday prayer habits.

2. Pastors and other spiritual leaders will be equipped to train others in the seven effective prayer habits.

3. Those completing the course will be able to pray comfortably and meaningfully with others in a small or large group setting.

Why the *Seven Habits* Course Works
Class Members:
1. **Are Convinced by the Word**
   Class participants, working on their own, delve into selected Scripture passages that describe one of the seven prayer habits. They are convicted by Scripture as they use **discover**, **reflect** and **apply** questions to dig out the meaning of the passages, under the guidance of the Holy Spirit.

2. **Learn from Each Other**
   Participants learn from each other each week in the class setting as the message of each Bible passage is discovered, interpreted and applied by the whole group.

3. **Take Important First Steps**
   Class members take important first prayer-habit steps in class. These set-aside times help them launch (or re-launch) each prayer habit. Members also spend time uncovering and dealing with habits that may hinder their prayer lives.

4. **Prayerfully Walk Together**
   Course participants walk together in prayer as they contribute to group prayer, pray with and for each other in small groups, and pray for each other between class sessions.

5. **Practice the Prayer Habits**
   Habits are only learned by persistent repetition. Students practice the prayer habits they are learning between weekly class sessions and throughout the nine-week course.

6. **Make the Prayer Habits Their Own**
   Class members, having gained proficiency in prayer habits, use what they have learned in the *Seven Habits* course to develop prayer devotional habits that are uniquely their own.

Outcomes of the *Seven Habits* Course

1. **Personal Life Transformation**
   Individual lives are transformed as good prayer habits lead to a closer walk with God, victory over sin, and abundant life in Christ.

2. **Increased Family Blessings**
   Parents who have strong prayer habits will not only release power and grace into the lives of their children, but will model these habits to their children, and will lead their families in meaningful family prayer times.

3. **More Prayer-Devoted Believers**
   The *Seven Habits* course is meant to be replicated. Class members become leaders of new groups. Pastors train their staffs. Youth pastors lead teen groups. Home group leaders take the course to their groups. Existing church teams—prayer teams, worship teams, education teams, outreach teams—do the course together. The end result will be more and more prayer-devoted believers.

4. **Affinity Group Prayer Support**
   Affinity groups are small groups who come together around a common interest. Believers with good prayer habits will find it very natural and desirable to find others with whom to pray. Whatever draws them together becomes the focus of their mutual prayers. (See **About the Course** appendix, "Finding an Affinity Prayer Group.")

5. **Enhanced Church Prayer Meetings**
   The more comfortable people are in praying with others the more likely they will be drawn to the church's regular prayer meetings, and to make positive contributions.

6. **Greater Effectiveness in Ministry**
   Effectiveness in ministry depends on prayer. Churches with increased numbers of prayer-devoted members will do the "even greater things" that Jesus spoke of in John 14:12-14. They should also expect to see more people "be saved and come to a knowledge of the truth" (1 Tim. 2:1-4).

Appendix

About the Course

Honing Your Prayer Habits

Understanding Prayer Habits

Webster's dictionary defines a habit as "a usual way of doing something." A *prayer* habit is a usual way of praying—or, better yet, **a usual way of relating to God**. All of us already have prayer habits. Some of these are good; others may not be so good. The purpose of this course is to help you develop habits of relating to God that will help you grow strong and effective in prayer and reap the rich harvest of spiritual blessings that will follow.

Developing good prayer habits **will require lots of practice**. Prayer habits are primarily habits of action, which can only be fully developed by means of ongoing practice. As aspiring athletes know, it is practice, practice, and more practice that finally leads to victory in athletic competition. Prayer habits too require practice if they are to yield spiritual victories. In the end you will have effective prayer habits not because you have finished the *Seven Habits* course but because you have practiced them to the point where they have become a normal part of your life.

Developing good prayer habits **is not easy**. It will be an uphill battle. Bad habits are hard to break. New habits are hard to form, especially if they go against the grain of our lives and our culture, as some prayer habits do. The devil is going to come against your attempts to form new prayer habits with everything in his arsenal. He doesn't want you to have the spiritual vitality and strength that come from a robust prayer life. Samuel Smiles understood the importance of paying attention to habits. He said, "Sow a thought, and you reap an act; sow an act, and you reap a habit; sow a habit, and you reap a character; sow a character, and you reap a destiny." You want the character of Christ and the destiny that goes with knowing him. Don't give up on the pursuit of good prayer habits once you finish the course. Press on! Press on against the push-back activities of our culture. Press on, if necessary, against the inclinations of your own "fleshly" nature. "Press on toward the goal to win the prize for which God has called [you] heavenward in Christ Jesus" (Phil. 3:14).

Each new prayer habit **will require a different approach**. For example, to develop the habit of *claiming God's riches* you may want to memorize key promise Scriptures like Matthew 7:7-8 and 1 John 5:14-15, and become very familiar with the Scripture verses that list the virtues and spiritual riches you want to claim (Galatians 4:22-23 – fruit, Ephesians 6:10-18 – armor, Colossians 3:12 – clothing, and 2 Peter 1:5-8—additives). On the other hand, to develop the *face-to-face with God* habit, you might need to set aside a daily time to meet God early in the morning and quietly sing some one-on-One songs like "Turn Your Eyes upon Jesus," or "O Lord, You're Beautiful." To *win over sin* you might find yourself mentally putting on the armor that Paul describes in Ephesians 6:10-17. Try to discover an approach to developing a prayer habit that is right for you.

First Steps in Honing Prayer Habits

1. Start by using the *Seven Habits Prayer Guide* found in the **Personal Guides** section of the Appendix. (You have permission to copy this page for personal use.) Keep it in an obvious place and pray through it often. This will be your way of saying, "God, I can't develop these habits on my own; I need your strength. Please help me to break hindering habits and to lock in the most helpful prayer habits."

2. Memorize and periodically review the *Memory Verses for the Seven Habits Course.* Let the Spirit speak to you through each of these verses and remind you of his intent for your prayer life.

3. Thoughtfully reread and meditate on key Scriptures in the seven prayer habits sessions. Review the *Summing Up* paragraphs and think through the **Four Steps to Develop the Habit**. Recommit yourself to God's high standard for devotion to prayer.

4. Review the *Ways to Develop the Prayer Habit* at the end of each session. Mark the ways that you think will best help you, and try the most likely ones first.

Next Steps in Honing Prayer Habits

1. **Focus on one prayer habit at a time.** Thank God for the prayer habits you have. Decide which new prayer habits are most important for you right now. Which are the most doable? Work on those first. Ask yourself questions like these: What is hindering my progress? Is there a slice of time in my day that I could use to better advantage? What strengths or passions can I build on? Is there a Bible verse I should memorize to reinforce this prayer habit?

2. **Get into a prayer support group.** Connect, if you can, with other believers in a prayer support group or an affinity prayer group. Agree to hold each other accountable for goals you've set. Meet regularly in order to pray for and with each other, and to share answers to prayer.

3. **Ask God to search you and to know your heart** at the end of each day to see if you have failed in prayer. Since the Spirit mandates us to pray "on all occasions, with all kinds of prayers and requests" and to "always keep on praying for all the saints," a daily review is fitting. Keep asking questions like these:

    - Am I experiencing more and more of God's blessings as I *claim his riches* each day?
    - What's happening in my relationship with God as I spend significant time *giving him glory* each day?
    - Am I really getting *face-to-face time* with God? Is this helping me be more conscious of God throughout each day?

- Am I *winning over sin* and gaining victories over the world, the flesh and the devil every day?
- Have I been able to *hear God's voice* and enjoy conversation with him today?
- Do I really have a sense of co-laboring with God on behalf of *other believers* that I care about, and am I making a difference in their lives?
- Am I getting more and more of God's heart for my *neighbors and the nations* of the world?

4. **Celebrate the gains you are making.** It's natural to focus on flaws and failures. It may be more helpful to notice improvements and to celebrate those. Thank God for successes, even small ones, and build on what you have achieved.

Appendix
About the Course

Finding an Affinity Prayer Group

An affinity prayer group is a small group of people who come together for prayer around a common interest. They may have similar personal or family needs, be in the same vocation, share a related ministry, or have a common vision or passion. Whatever draws them together becomes the focus of their prayers. They pray with and for each other. Though prayer is their primary focus, they will often be found putting legs to their prayers by ministering together. In other words, the prayer group may become a prayer/action group.

Affinity prayer groups are usually small—three to five persons. Praying together in a small group is more comfortable than in a large group and allows deeper sharing and personal intimacy. Members give each other a lot of support and can become very intimate. For this reason most affinity prayer groups are same-sex groups.

Affinity prayer groups tend to fit the culture of our day. Believers with busy schedules and complicated lives are more likely to find convenient times and places to meet if the group is small and their times flexible. They may even choose to pray together by telephone conference or Google Hang-Out and can keep each other updated between meeting times by e-mail or text messaging.

Following are several types of affinity prayer groups:

- **Spiritual Formation Group**

    One of the best ways to foster personal spiritual growth is to be part of a small accountability group where members regularly study the Bible together, share the ups and downs their spiritual journeys, and pray for each other. Even Jesus had his inner three—the disciples he took with him onto the Mount of Transfiguration and into the bitter trials of Gethsemane. A spiritual formation group may be just the kind of group to support believers who are struggling in their marriages, tempted or tested in a work situation, or straining at the responsibilities of ministry.

- **Health Care Prayer Group**

    A health care prayer group may be a group of health care workers or simply persons who have health concerns or a strong interest in health. They may pray about group members' illnesses or disabilities, or health problems of extended family members and the larger Christian community. These health issues may be physical or emotional, long-term or short-term. This group may even become a mobile prayer team that goes to hospitals, long-term care facilities, personal residences or other locations to pray with people.

- **Parents in Prayer**

    Parents who come together in an affinity prayer group may do so in order to pray for themselves or for their children. They may share a special concern for children at a certain age level or wrestle over the spiritual well-being of sons or daughters who are spiritually unresponsive. Foster parents, parents with adopted children, and parents with special-needs children often find that they have a common bond and shared concerns over which to pray.

- **Spouses in Prayer**

    Marriage partners come together to share their personal burdens in a relationship and/or to labor in behalf of their spouses. They may have a concern about the physical, emotional or spiritual well-being of a spouse, or even a former spouse. They pray for sustaining and transforming grace.

- **Celebrate Recovery Prayer Group**

    Persons who have recovered from an addiction (or who are in the process of recovering) usually require a great deal of prayer support. Believers who have walked a similar path are the very ones who will best understand and will be most able to pray with intensity and focus. This is also true for those who have suffered abuse. A celebrate-recovery group is not meant to substitute for needed therapy, but will surely be a significant factor in any full-scale recovery process.

- **Seek God for My Church**

    Any church would be blessed by having one or more affinity prayer groups praying for the leaders, ministries and members of that church. You could, for example, pray for

    ◊ A healthy and unified church like those mentioned in Acts 2:42 and John 17:23

    ◊ Godly leaders like those mentioned in Acts 20:28

    ◊ Spiritual worship such as Jesus envisioned in John 4:23-24

    ◊ Christian education rooted in Deuteronomy 6:7, 2 Timothy 3:16-17 and Philippians 4:8

    ◊ Fellowship and hospitality resembling that mentioned in Hebrews 13:2 and 1 Peter 4:9

    ◊ Spirit-enabled prayer, reflecting Ephesians 6:18 and 1 Timothy 2:1-4

    ◊ Outreach prompted by Matthew 28:19-20, Acts 1:8 and Matthew 5:16

    ◊ Spiritual growth like that which Paul prayed for in Ephesians 3:14-20 and Philippians 1:9-11.

    If there were more than one group of this type, it would be natural for them to come together from time to time for large group prayer.

- **Seek God for the Unsaved**

    Persons with the spiritual gift of evangelism and those who have a passion for seeing lost friends, family members, neighbors and coworkers come to Christ will feel comfortable coming together to pray for the unsaved. The Billy Graham Evangelistic Association perfected the very effective triplet model of praying for unsaved persons in advance of the Graham crusades.

    In this model a small prayer group of three each brings the names of several unbelievers to the attention of their group. The triplets meet weekly to pray for each other and for the unbelievers they have identified. They also pray for opportunities to witness to those they are praying for. This method has subsequently been used successfully in many churches. The following Bible passages may help this kind of group focus their prayers along Scriptural lines:

- ◊ Pray that unsaved persons you pray for will be drawn to Christ (Jn. 6:44).
- ◊ Pray that their eyes will be open to see the light of the gospel (2 Cor. 4:4).
- ◊ Pray that those who hear the gospel will understand it (Matt. 13:19).
- ◊ Pray that they will be given the faith to believe (Mk. 2:1-5).

- **Seek God for the Campus**

    Those attracted to this kind of affinity group may be parents of students, faculty or staff at the school, youth leaders in the church, or simply those with a burden for good education. The campus they pray over may be that of a local grade school, high school, college or university, where people they know and care about are involved as faculty or students. Intercessors in this kind of group will want to ramp up prayer at special times of the year such as opening day, test periods, graduations, and so on. Attending school functions, prayer walks, and prayer drives will help keep intercessors focused. Pray-ers in this group may want to pray Scriptures like Deuteronomy 5:16, Psalm 119:9, Proverbs 22:6, Ecclesiastes 12:1 and 1 John 2:13-14.

- **Seek God for Your City**

    Jesus challenged his disciples to "seek first the kingdom of God." That means that we are to do everything possible to instill God's concerns into the governmental structures of the towns and cities where we live and do business. Kingdom Christians work for social justice, poverty relief, suitable health care, good education, strong families, favorable business environments, affordable housing, racial equality, and religious freedom. This kind of prayer group can be an important first step in addressing local governmental issues.

- **Teens in Prayer**

    Teens will bring a lot of energy to an affinity group focused on the issues of their complex lives. Many have deep concerns for friends who are making unhealthy life choices. Some will want to pray about future life partners. Others have questions about future college and career choices. All of them will desire to claim for themselves and others the rich promises of God as they grow in Christ.

- **Seniors in Prayer**

    Seniors, especially believers who have had many years of faith and service, will often be the most faithful and powerful intercessors in the church. Though less able to do the kinds of things that require youthful strength and endurance, they may "*still bear fruit in old age, they will stay fresh and green.*" Their powerful prayers may strengthen growing grandchildren who are facing new and tempting situations, support missionaries who serve in challenging environments, or stimulate spiritual growth in younger believers. Seniors may find prayer partners in their home church, in a retirement facility, or in their complex or neighborhood.

Create Your Own Group

If you do not find in the list above a type of group that fits your needs or interests, consider creating a group that fits you and your world of experience. Following are some other possible types of groups:

- ◊ A ministry group that focuses on Christian education, outreach, worship, hospitality, or social needs
- ◊ A social issue group that concentrates on abortion issues, adoption, poverty, dysfunctional families, homelessness, sex trafficking, or some kind of discrimination
- ◊ A work-related group that supports those in law enforcement, social work, health care, government services, media, business owners, or clergy roles.

Appendix

About the Course

Becoming a Prayer-Devoted Church

In the first session of this *Seven Habits* course you studied a number of Scripture passages that depicted the early church as a prayer-devoted church. Now that you have finished the course, it is time to ask again the question "How can our church become more devoted to prayer?" Or, more specifically, "How can those who've completed this course help our congregation become more devoted to prayer?" What follows are some answers to that question.

How *Graduates* Can Develop Devotion to Prayer at Their Church

1. **Continue to Refine Effective Prayer Habits**
   Review the appendix chapter on *Honing Your Prayer Habits* with other class members, emphasizing the importance of ongoing practice. Be aware of the many distractions and hindrances you face in trying to develop good prayer habits. Make plans to overcome the hindrances and continue to grow.

2. **Become Part of an Affinity Prayer Group**
   Review together the basic ideas in the appendix chapter on *Affinity Prayer Groups*. Think and pray about becoming part of an affinity prayer group. You might even want to try it for three or four weeks with a couple of people before you make a long-term commitment.

3. **Pray for Future *Seven Habits* Course Participants**
   No one is better positioned to pray for future *Seven Habits* course participants than those who have completed the course. Think about persons in your church who would be most likely to benefit from this course, and pray that they will respond favorably to an invitation.

4. **Tell Others about the *Seven Habits* Course**
   Few are likely to sign up for a nine-week prayer course just because it is mentioned in the church bulletin. The majority of those who take the course in the future will be those whose interest has been quickened by the inspiring testimony of a course graduate. That means that those who have taken and benefited from the course will be on the frontlines of future promotion efforts.

5. **Consider Leading a *Seven Habits* Course**
   The *Seven Habits* course is based primarily on inductive Bible study. Even if you are uncomfortable in an upfront leadership role, you can effectively lead inductive studies. Think about future possible groups and those who may lead them. Think and pray about the possibility of leading a *Seven Habits* class yourself in the future.

How *Pastors and Church Staff* Can Develop Devotion to Prayer

1. **Continue to Offer and Lead *Seven Habits* Classes**
   All true Christians pray, but not all have well-developed prayer lives. Don't assume that people will pray more just because they are given the opportunity or are challenged to do so. Most Christians need to be taught about prayer and given help in practical aspects of prayer, if they are to grow strong and effective. Many Christians are unsatisfied with their prayer lives and, given the time and opportunity, will accept the help you can offer them by means of the *Seven Habits* course. The ultimate goal is not simply to teach the course successfully but to help as many members of the church as possible develop devoted prayer lives.

2. **Give All Staff Members Prayer Support**
   If it is true, as Peter Wagner says, that "the most underutilized source of spiritual power in our churches today is intercession for spiritual leaders," then finding and recruiting prayer partners for all staff members is crucial. The grace and power that prayer support teams are able to release into staff members' lives and ministries will bless the whole congregation.

3. **Train the Church's Key Leaders**
   If church staff members, board members, small group leaders, and committee chair persons have not taken the *Seven Habits* course, then the pastor should plan to lead the course for these types of leaders. No church will become truly devoted to prayer unless the majority of its key leaders have strong and healthy prayer lives.

4. **Increase Prayer Time in Leadership Meetings**
   Some church councils, boards and committees spend up to half of their regular meeting times in prayer. Almost without exception, these groups testify that increased amounts of time spent in prayer result in shorter meetings. How is this possible? Because increased prayer brings definitive divine guidance, a clearer sense of direction, and greater unity.

5. **Focus Worship Prayer Times on God's Kingdom Vision**
   It may seem expedient to fill the congregational prayer time in a worship service with the personal needs and concerns of the membership. However, a steady diet of such prayers sends a truncated message about prayer to those gathered in worship. It suggests that God is our servant and prayer is the way to get him to do our bidding. Kingdom-oriented prayers, on the other hand, convey the truth that God is building his kingdom and pursuing his purposes in response to the prayers of his people.

What *Key Lay Leaders* Can Do to Develop Devotion to Prayer

1. **Appoint and Mandate a Prayer Leadership Team**
   Local church prayer ministries need leadership. As more members develop effective prayer lives, there will be increasing need for a prayer leadership team to organize and support the congregation's prayer activities . Members of this team should have gifts of leadership, and organization and communication skills coupled with a passion for prayer. The team should operate within the infrastructure of the church. The following steps may be among the first things that a prayer leadership team can accomplish.

2. **Provide Prayer Support for Worship**
   Worship is at the heart of a congregation's spiritual life. Powerful and effective prayer for worship will lift the spiritual energy level in worship and affect the lives of worshipers. God wants to bless the hearts of worshipers and to grow them in grace and in knowledge. He wants to freshly anoint the preacher, inspire the worship leaders, and enhance the spirit of love and fellowship for all his people. God chooses to do these kinds of things in response to our *asking*. Intercessors who pray before and during worship have a high calling.

3. **Provide Prayer Covering for Those In Ministry**
   In most churches a minority of the members do a majority of the work. That minority deserves to be well supported in prayer. Try to provide a prayer partner for everyone involved in ministry in or for the church. Doing so will increase the effectiveness of those in ministry. It will also give prayer partners a way to make a vital contribution to the church and to appreciate the ministries they are undergirding in prayer.

4. **Communicate Prayer Requests and Answers**
   To be effective in prayer people need to know who and what to pray for. If you regularly communicate prayer needs, answers to prayer, and opportunities for prayer you will increase both the amount and the effectiveness of prayer in your church. Be sure that, in addition to health issues and personal concerns, you communicate kingdom concerns and the vision of the church, as well as the needs of your community and your nation.

5. **Integrate More Prayer Into Corporate Activities**
   Prayer should be a priority in every church activity. This means more than opening and closing activities in prayer. It may mean inviting all who are gathered to contribute to a prayer. It may mean delaying discussion in order to wrestle in prayer over an issue. It may mean praying through a passage of Scripture or silently waiting on the Spirit. Above all, it will mean becoming conscious of God's presence, guidance and protection in whatever we are being called to do. That happens best through prayer.

6. **Plan a Whole-Church Prayer Initiative**
   Many churches have successfully involved their members in a church-wide prayer initiative in which weekly sermons, small-group Bible studies, and personal and/or family devotions are all focused on prayer for a period of time, often for forty days. These churches have been able to take significant strides forward. (A *40-Days of Prayer Resource Kit* with sermon outlines, small-group resources and devotional reading material is available from Harvest Prayer Ministries. See www.harvestprayer.com for more information on this resource.)

What to Expect As Your Church Becomes More Fully Devoted to Prayer

1. **Increased Effectiveness in Ministry**
   Jesus linked effective ministry to prayer. He assured his disciples that they would do what he had done and "even greater things," because he was going to the Father and would do whatever they asked in his name (Jn. 14:12-14). Increased effectiveness in prayer will increase effectiveness in your church's ministries.

2. **Greater Spiritual Protection**
   Jesus regularly connected prayer and spiritual protection. He taught us a pattern for prayer that ended with "deliver us from the evil one" (Matt. 6:13). Twice he secured protection for his disciples in his pre-crucifixion prayer recorded in John 17. In Gethsemane he urged his sleeping disciples to "watch and pray so that you will not fall into temptation" (Matt. 26:41). Paul challenged all believers to be alert to the devil's schemes and to "always keep on praying for all God's people" (Eph. 6:18). A prayer-devoted church will surely experience much greater protection from forces of evil than a prayer-apathetic congregation.

3. **Effective Evangelism and Discipleship**
   Paul urged young Pastor Timothy to make sure that "requests, prayers, intercession and thanksgiving be made for everyone.... This is good and pleases God our Savior, who wants all persons to be saved and to come to a knowledge of the truth" (1 Tim. 2:1, 3-4). In other words prayer will be a key factor in bringing people to salvation and growth in knowledge of the truth.

4. **An Upsurge in Social Transformation**
   Speaking through the prophet Jeremiah, God challenged Jewish exiles on their way to captivity in Babylon to "seek the peace and prosperity of the city to which I have carried you into exile. Pray to the Lord for it, because if it prospers, you too will prosper" (Jer. 29:7). He was saying that prayer for the well-being of the city would make so much difference that they themselves, though exiles in a foreign land, would be blessed in the wake of the impact that prayer would make. Paul also taught his readers that their prayers "for kings and all those in authority" in the Roman world would make it possible for all to live "peaceful and quiet lives in all godliness and holiness" (1 Tim. 2:1-2).

Appendix

About the Course

Bonus Follow-Up Session

> **Note:** If a *Seven Habits* class decides to meet for the *Bonus Follow-up Session* described below, set a date (_____), time (_____), and place (_____) for this meeting at the end of Session 9.

The *Bonus Follow-Up Session* is an optional future session—not a final exam or a way to check up on how well members have done, but rather an opportunity for members to encourage each other and share the benefits gained from a more effective prayer life.

Though this session is optional, it is really quite important, simply because we are talking about habits, which take practice—sometimes a lot of practice over time. Habits don't get locked in after just nine weeks.

This session is also a valuable opportunity to learn what has helped other members grow in prayer, and to share with them insights that will help them grow stronger in prayer. The devil is doing everything in his power to keep your group members from the habits of a robust prayer life. You need to do everything possible to support each in this spiritual growth process and to frustrate the efforts of the evil one. This session is one way to do that.

The questions in this session assume some familiarity with the appendix chapters, especially "Honing Your Prayer Habits", "Finding an Affinity Prayer Group", and "Becoming a Prayer-Devoted Church"—chapters intended to help members continue to grow strong prayer lives. Review these chapters before the bonus session. The share questions below are divided into three groups: the *practice* of prayer habits, the *results* of specific prayer habits, and the *future plans* for prayer habits. The session will end with an unstructured group prayer time.

Share Questions on the <u>Practice</u> of *Seven Habits of Prayer*

1. What has been happening in your prayer life since you have taken the *Seven Habits* course?

2. Has the amount of time that you spend in prayer increased?

3. Has your understanding of prayer changed?

4. Which prayer habits have made the most difference in your prayer life? Which have been the most difficult?

5. Have you found the *Prayer Guide* or the *Memory Verses Guide* (located in

Share Questions on the *Results* of Specific *Habits of Prayer*

1. Do you have a sense that you have received **spiritual riches** because you have asked for them?

2. Do you find yourself taking greater delight in God as you regularly **give him glory**?

3. What happens when you go **face-to-face** with God?

4. Have you been **winning** more battles over the world, the flesh, and the devil as you have prayed for victory?

5. Have you had any surprising, or not so surprising, experiences in **hearing God's voice**?

6. Have you noticed your prayers making a difference in the lives of **other believers**?

7. What difference did your prayers for **neighbors or nations** make in your feelings toward them?

8. Have you seen any changes in devotion to **prayer at your church**? Has praying *with* others become easier or more meaningful for you?

Share Questions on *Future Plans* with *Habits of Prayer*

1. What do you hope to do in the future to hone your prayer habits?

2. Have you found a prayer support or an affinity group with whom to pray regularly?

3. Are there some additional ways that you would like to contribute to prayer at your church?

4. Have you thought about leading a *Seven Habits* prayer class in the future?

Final Prayer Time

As a whole group, *focus your prayer time mostly on prayer itself* - prayer that claims God's riches, gives God glory, meets him face to face, hears his voice, wins over sin, makes a difference in the lives of others, and permeates your church.

Appendix

Leader Helps

How to Use This Course

Three Ways to Use This Course

1. **A Nine-Week Course with Ninety-Minute Sessions**
   In a ninety-minute *Seven Habits* session, members spend the first minutes sharing their prayer-habit experience of the past week with the class, then 45 minutes on the Bible study, and the rest of the time in personal, small group and whole group activities to develop the prayer habits.

2. **A Nine-Week Course with Fifty-Minute Session**
   In a fifty-minute *Seven Habits* session, members spend about half of the class time on the Bible study and the other half on the exercises to develop the prayer habits.

3. **Nine Sessions in a Two-to-Three-Day Retreat**
   The *Seven Habits* course also works well as the curriculum for a two-to-three-day spiritual retreat. Busy people, who often have to fight schedules to have time for the course work, particularly appreciate this model.

Appendix
Leader Helps

Forming a *Seven Habits* Class

Choosing Class Members
Ask God to show you whom to invite into your *Seven Habits* class. Church leaders will want to consider especially those in key leadership roles: staff, council, board members and trustees. Also, look for those who have the potential to lead similar groups in the future. Those who are already in prayer groups will be among those who have the highest interest, particularly if they are strong in some habits of prayer and want help to develop others.

Limit the Class Size
Plan for a group of nine to twelve members. Remember that this is an inductive Bible study. The learning process depends on personal participation in a small group setting. Large numbers simply do not work well.

The Exploratory Meeting
In some situations you may want to invite a group of possible participants to an exploratory meeting in which you show them the course manual, give them a preview of the course content, and underscore the importance of preparing for and attending the classes and practicing the prayer habits. Describe the benefits of the course and explain the need to continue practicing the habits even after the course is completed. Note that this training will prepare them to be part of prayer affinity group in the future. This meeting may also be the time to give them the *Seven Habits* course manual so they can prepare for the first regular class session.

Time and Place of Meeting
Review possible meeting times with the group. Invite their input. Settle on a time and place to meet, and set a starting date.

Class Member Commitment
Encourage potential class members to pray about taking the course and to let you know if they plan to attend.

Future *Seven Habits* Course Leaders
As your class progresses be on the lookout for class members who seem capable of leading a *Seven Habits* class in the future. Speak to them partway through the course about leading their own class. If they appear interested, encourage them to review the steps above and to start their own list of potential class members.

Appendix

Leader Helps

Leading a *Seven Habits* Class

ADVANCE PREPARATON
If you have not taken the course as a participant, it would be wise to go through the course on your own before leading others through it. This will enable to share your own prayer-habit experiences with the class you lead. Be prepared to share any struggles you may have in developing the habits, as well as your success experiences.

Go through the course by reading the opening paragraphs, studying the Scriptures, reflecting on the questions, and practicing each prayer habit.

Review the four **After the Course** appendices chapters: "Honing Your Prayer Habits," "Finding an Affinity Prayer Group," "Becoming a Prayer-Devoted Church" and the "Bonus Session" in order to be aware upfront of what can and should happen after your group finishes the course.

LEADING THE CLASS
Opening Prayer
Open each class session with a prayer (led by you or a class member) that reflects what you have learned and practiced in the past week, and what lies ahead in your class time.

Sharing Time (5-7 minutes)
If you are leading a 90-minute class, use some time at the beginning of each class session (except Session One) for class members to share, in a couple of sentences, one prayer-habit experience from the past week. All class members should benefit from these sharings. (You will not have time for this experience in a 50-minute class session.)

Bible Study
- Introduce each session with a two- to three-minute reflection on the topic of that session. Pick up on a thought from the opening paragraphs or reflect on your own experience with this prayer habit.

- Lead the class through the inductive Bible study time, one section at a time. First, invite class members to participate in reading the Scripture portions out loud. Then go through the questions, inviting class members to share their thoughts and insights. You don't have to use all the questions. Try to make use of the questions that have yielded the best insights for you or them. (50-minute groups will have 5-7 minutes for each subsection.)

- End the Bible study by having class member reflect on the two *Bottom Line Questions*. These questions will help class members assess the overall impact of each lesson and apply what they have learned to their own prayer lives.

Summing Up
The *Summing Up* segment provides a brief summary of the biblical truths just studied and unpacks some of the implications of these truths for our prayer lives. Review this section briefly with the class, underscoring the ideas that are most important for your group.

Four Steps to Develop the Habit

This is a *very* important section in each of the *Seven Habits* sessions. Here's why! This is the time when class members are challenged to think seriously about actually developing the prayer habit they have just studied. The first three steps in this segment—setting the stage, detecting hindering habits, and launching the habit—require personal involvement and are intended to *jumpstart* the process of forming a prayer habit. Lead the class through the first three steps, one at a time, giving them 3-4 minutes per step. (You may wish to preview these steps with the class the first time through.) Use step 4 to challenge them to do the kinds of things that will help them translate the truths learned into a habit. Use your own experience as an example.

Group Prayer and Covenant Time

Pace the class through the three activities in this section one step at a time. Give them a small amount of time to do the first and second step. Then encourage each person in the class to pray a two-sentence prayer in the whole-group prayer time. This is a time for those who are fearful of praying aloud in a group to take baby steps in that direction. For those who find this difficult, you may suggest that they simply read what they have written in step two. Some may delay contributing to whole-group prayer until the later sessions. (You, as leader, should pray first in this whole group prayer time in order to model a brief two sentence prayer, and to give class members an example of confessing a hindering habit and claiming the grace for a "right" prayer habit.)

Close this group prayer time by moving directly into the *Whole Group Covenant*.

Small Group Share and Prayer Time

Introduce the small group share and prayer time. Review the three elements in this section briefly. (This will only be necessary for the first one or two sessions.) Give them a minute or two to write something down in the blanks related with the first arrow tip.

Make **looking-ahead comments** at this time: next week's theme, meeting time, etc. (This is your last chance to speak to the whole group since they will be free to leave on their own after the small group prayer time.) Stress the importance of **Praying for Each Other** and **Praying About Their Prayer Lives**. Remind them of the helpful suggestions in the **Develop the Habit** section.

Suggest some way for them to divide into small groups of 2-4. (Allow those who have found good small group prayer partners in the first couple of weeks to stay together as a small group for the rest of the course.) Free them to move into small groups for the share and prayer time. Allow them to spread around the room and to do their sharing and praying either sitting or standing. Let them knows that they free to leave when they have finished their share and prayer times together.

AT THE END OF THE COURSE

- Encourage them to pray for other class members for at least one month beyond the last session.

- Call attention to the *Seven Habits* **Prayer Guide** and the **Memory Verses** for the *Seven Habits* Course, and highlight the value of using these guides to reinforce the habits of prayer.

- Urge them to review all the sessions of the course in the next month, giving special attention to the opening paragraphs of each session, and to the "Lock in the Habit" suggestions at the end of the "Four Steps to Develop the Prayer Habit" section of each session.

- Draw attention to second, third, and fourth chapters in the **About the Course** section of the appendices: **Honing Your Prayer Habits, Finding an Affinity Prayer Group,** and **Becoming a Prayer-Devoted Church** and encourage them to make use of the suggestions in these chapters to continue growing their prayer lives and to help their church to become more devoted to prayer.

- Encourage them to promote the *Seven Habits* course among their friends-in-Christ by sharing how the course has helped them grow stronger in prayer.

- Give the class a few minutes to think about coming back together after several weeks for the **Bonus Session.** If there is interest in this, set a tentative time. Then follow through.

Appendix

Personal Guides

Seven Habits Prayer Guide

Jesus, I want to be a Christian who, like you and your early disciples, is **devoted to prayer**. Help me to *pray in the Spirit on all occasions with all kinds of prayer,* and to *pray devotedly for all God's people.* (Eph. 6:18)

Lord, help me learn to **claim spiritual riches** by constantly *asking, seeking and knocking* so that I may *receive, find, and get an open door* to the blessings that you offer me. (Matt. 7:7-8)

Jesus, I really want to *continually offer to God a sacrifice of praise—the fruit of lips that openly profess your name.* Give me a praising heart so that I may **give you glory** *as long as I live.* (Heb. 13:15, Ps. 146:2)

Lord, you have said, "*Seek my face.*" My heart says: "*Your face, Lord, I seek.*" Give me a *soul that yearns for you,* a *spirit that earnestly seeks you.* Teach me, Lord, how to **seek your face**, so that I may enjoy delightful one-on-One times with you. (Ps. 27:8)

Lord, I truly want to **win over sin**. Pardon my sins and forgive my transgressions. Give me the desire and the ability to continually *crucify the flesh,* overcome the world, and *resist the devil.* (Mic. 7:18, Rom. 8:13, 1 Jn. 5:4-5, Jas. 4:7)

Jesus, I know that you want me to live by *every word that comes from the mouth of God,* just as you did. Give me the *Spirit of wisdom and revelation* so that I may **hear your voice**, *may know you better and may have the eyes of my heart enlightened.* (Mt. 4:4, Jn. 12:50, Eph. 1:17)

Lord, I pray for my **family and friends in Christ**. *Strengthen them with power through your Spirit in their inner being so that you may dwell in their hearts through faith. I pray that they may be rooted and grounded in God's love so that they will know and personally experience the far-reaching love of Christ* and *be filled to the measure of the fullness of God.* (Eph. 3:14-19)

Lord, hear me as I make *requests, prayers, intercession and thanksgiving for all people*—for my **neighbors and for nations**, as well as government leaders. I know that *this is good and pleases* you; and that you *want all people to be saved and to come to a knowledge of the truth.* (1 Tim. 2:1-4)

Lord, I pray that my church will be **a prayer-devoted church**, that is both watchful and thankful. Help me to find ways to encourage devotion to prayer.

*Permission is granted to copy this page for personal use.

Appendix

Personal Guides

Memory Verses for the *Seven Habits* Course

Devote yourself to prayer, and keep the *Seven Habits of Effective Prayer* in mind, by memorizing and regularly reviewing the following verses.

My Desire: Be a Prayer-Devoted Christian
And pray in the Spirit on all occasions with all kinds of prayers and requests. With this in mind, be alert and always keep on praying for all the Lord's people. –Eph. 6:18

Habit One: Claim God's Riches
This is the confidence we have in approaching God: that if we ask anything according to his will, he hears us. And if we know that he hears us—whatever we ask—we know that we have what we asked of him. –1 Jn. 5:14-15

Habit Two: Give God Glory
Oh, the depth of the riches of the wisdom and knowledge of God! How unsearchable his judgments, and his paths beyond tracing out! "Who has known the mind of the Lord? Or who has been his counselor?" "Who has ever given to God, that God should repay them?" For from him and through him and for him are all things. To him be the glory forever! –Rom. 11:33-36

Habit Three: Seek God's Face
You make known to me the path of life; you will fill me with joy in your presence, with eternal pleasures at your right hand. –Ps. 16:11

Habit Four: Win over Sin
"Watch and pray so that you will not fall into temptation. The spirit is willing, but the flesh is weak." –Matt. 26:41

Habit Five: Hear God's Voice
"My sheep listen to my voice; I know them, and they follow me." –Jn. 10:27

Habit Six: Pray Family and Friends in Christ
Pray for each other. . . .The prayer of a righteous person is powerful and effective. –Js. 5:16

Habit Seven: Pray for Neighbors and Nations
I urge, then, first of all, that petitions, prayers, intercession and thanksgiving be made for all people—for kings and all those in authority, that we may live peaceful and quiet lives in all godliness and holiness. This is good, and pleases God our Savior, who wants all people to be saved and to come to a knowledge of the truth. –1 Tim. 2:1-4

My Church: Be a Prayer-Devoted Church
Devote yourselves to prayer, being watchful and thankful. –Col. 4:2

---

*Permission is granted to copy this page for personal use.

www.ingramcontent.com/pod-product-compliance
Lightning Source LLC
Chambersburg PA
CBHW080413300426
44113CB00015B/2505